"You do not take a person who,
for years,
has been **hobbled by chains** *and* **liberate him,**
bring him up to the starting line of **a race**
and then say,
'You are free to compete with all the others,' and still justly believe that you have been **completely fair.***"*

-President Lyndon B. Johnson
June 4, 1965,
Howard University Commencement Address

What is the
400 year head start?

The 400 year head start refers to the 250 years of ***legal*** enslavement of black people and the 150 years of ***legal*** discrimination, which *intentionally* gave white people an advantage and black people a disadvantage to having access to opportunities in the United States of America.

The 400 Year Head Start

Yet Still Destined for Glory

Written by:
Nikki Ace

Dedicated to my children
-Wesley and Dani-
May you always run a winning race!

ISBN: 978-0-578-67148-2

Contents

Introduction

So, what I want you to do is imagine being in a race. It doesn't matter that you don't have running shoes or running attire.

You're in a race, so get to it!

Now, visualize being at the starting point of this race, but the other runner is so far ahead, you can hardly even see them. Finally, you start to run, but you notice that your lane is obviously different.

There are hurdles in your lane, so you jump. There are mountains in your lane, so you climb. There are walls in your lane, so you push through. And there are people literally pulling you back, so you fight.

With much contemplation, you realize this race would clearly be fair if all the lanes had these same barriers and challenges.

But they don't.

And this is the black experience.

I have recently had to rethink my black history. It has been over 400 years since Africans were forcibly brought to what would become the United States of America. To put it plainly, **1619** is most notably recorded as the year African captives were first sold into slavery when they arrived in the British colony of Jamestown, Virginia.

The history of black people is literally the history of America.

And although blacks have contributed so much to the development of this country, we have not been able to close the racial gap between white Americans and black Americans in areas such as wealth, education, access to quality healthcare, housing, etc . . .. And let me just remind you . . . it's been over 400 years!

Hence, 'The 400 Year Head Start'.

In schools, students don't spend enough time learning about black history and they are definitely not taught about this head start. However, students may learn little pieces of information about slavery. But slavery is not the beginning of black history as it is made out to be. Black history began in Africa.

Like so many, I was **not** taught that Africa was a civilized, sophisticated and cultured continent prior to American slavery. It was believed to be a place where people - that were **not** socially, culturally or morally advanced- lived amongst the wild animals and was a land of nothing more than jungles, safaris and a "Lion King-ish" lifestyle.

I didn't know.

But had I known Africa's achievements, I would have loved myself more. I would have challenged myself to learn more about Africa's forgotten rich history, which is the origin of all life.

I would've also embraced the history of my ancestors experience during enslavement where they were given scraps or left overs to eat and how they cleverly turned these into delicacies.

To know that my predecessors protested, marched, were jailed and even died so that someone like me can enjoy all that America has to offer, just proves the dignity of black people. Although being stripped of their human rights, these black people saw the value in themselves and fought their best fight to be treated and respected as American citizens should.

I mean . . . just look at the words in the United States Declaration of Independence written by Thomas Jefferson:

> *"We hold these Truths to be self-evident, that* ***all Men are created equal,*** *that they are endowed by their Creator with certain unalienable Rights, that among these are Life, Liberty and the Pursuit of Happiness ... "*

Now, these words sound all fine and dandy, however this specific author actually owned multiple slaves himself. So, did he really believe that all men were created equal?

Even if he didn't believe in the humanity of the enslaved, enslaved black people did.

They believed in their right to be treated as human beings because they were created by the same Creator of mankind.

And they believed this so much, that they never stopped working...and fighting...and thriving with faith to experience the liberties and pursuit of happiness they deserve!

Sometimes the truth hurts. But does this mean we shouldn't tell the truth? Should we continue to keep what's in the dark hidden? The indignities that black people endured should not go on without notice.

I believe the truth included in this book will help towards the **building up and healing of black people.** There are wounds that are still open and these wounds still hurt.

I also believe the truth included in this book will help towards the **healing of relationships even between blacks and whites**:

****Black people will learn* that there were actually white people that fought in the struggle to emancipating black people, whether as an abolitionist, fighting and dying in the American

Civil War or marching and protesting during the Civil Rights Movement.

*** *White people will realize* that there are systems intentionally put in place by the *'corridors of power'* to continue to dehumanize blacks. They will also recognize that America's decision to enslave black people have left a 'residue' that continues to impact the overall quality of life for black people. (Note: I define the *'corridors of power'* as the highest level of authority mostly occupied by white people that are responsible for shaping the history of America.)

Many people will respond to this truth with pain.

Others may feel a sense of guilt.

Sympathetic readers will feel a sense of empathy.

And the *affirmatively ignorant* will deny all this history as history books had before.

Some people just don't want to know the truth:

***The truth is that the legacy of slavery still affects the quality of life for black people today.**

***The truth is** that the institution of slavery still has a ripple effect that impacts <u>all</u> Americans right here . . . right now.

*** **I have learned** that systemic injustices actually exist and that black people are still influenced by past practices.

*** **And I have learned** that racist stereotypes that originated from slavery, still has a way of rearing its ugly head in modern society. This influences the mindset and decisions of the '*powers that be*'.

Through my research, I learned that there are intergenerational transfers and transactions within the white community that black people have not been able to take advantage of.

White advantage is passed down from parent *to* child and from child *to* grandchild, consequently allowing them to have an enormous head start. While white people have been able to pass down wealth and opportunities to their families, blacks have not been afforded the same benefits.

This made it all so clear to me why there is so much of a disparity between the races.

To say the least, I am so happy that my children's inquisitiveness in their own black history reignited my interest in this subject. In order to feed their curiosity, I have been on a research frenzy.

Whether I watched TED Talks, YouTube videos, documentaries, or read sections in books, articles or blogs, I learned such a wealth of information. I wanted to offer my children accurate answers to the myriad of questions I know they may not receive in school.

This topic is emotionally taxing, which is probably why teachers stray away from teaching this truth. But one thing we also have to recognize is that it may not be that teachers don't want to teach the truth . . . they may not even know the truth for themselves. This is due to the fact that black history lessons are not mandated in the curriculum at most schools.

So, in order to appeal to the masses, I have written this book in *easy-to-read* language while explaining the truth of some landmark events in black history. These are some of the events that seemed to deliberately try to slow down or attempt to prevent the progress of black people.

This book's purpose is not to rehash anger and hatred towards those that have oppressed black people, but it is merely a tool to educate and expose an honest account of the black experience here in America.

For me, this new knowledge has helped me have more pride in who I am and I have gained so much more respect and appreciation for those who came before me. I am so grateful for my learning and I hope that you will become more dignified in this American history as well.

"Until the lion has a historian,
the hunter will always be the hero."

-African Proverb

Hurdle #1

The Capture

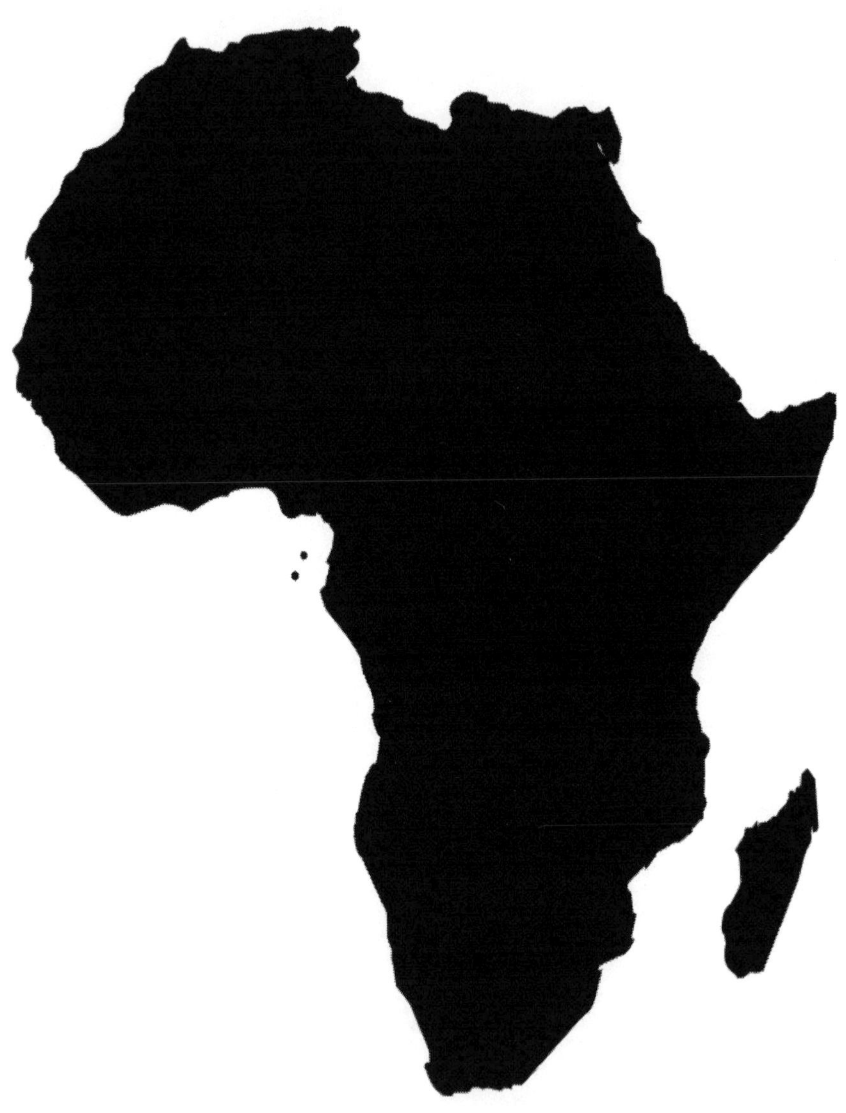

Kidnapped
and taken *involuntarily*,
Africans were stolen
from the land where beauty *bleeds*.

On ships, they set sail,
but none like a *cruise*.
Limited space had
person packed next to person like *spoons*.

For months and months,
they traveled on the vast *sea*,
malnourished and shackled
and beaten on *fleet*.

Millions were shipped
to far lands *unknown*.
To the Africans, the strange place
was clearly not *home*.

Fully conscious . . .
on purpose . . . and *deliberately,*
Africans were brought to
America's land of *unfamiliarity.*

They were defenseless on this land
without their known *resources,*
making it more important these now slaves
unite and join *forces.*

Fueled by greed,
expansion and *prosperity,*
Europeans did everything to try to
take the enslaved *humanity.*

They **intentionally stripped** them
from the place they call *home.*
Away from family these poor people
felt helpless and *alone.*

Being held captive,
no matter man, woman or *age,*
newborns, children to seniors
endured tremendous *pain.*

Once on America's soil,
with no relief from *exhaustion,*
Africans were put on display
for the slave traders *auction.*

They knew exactly
who they were putting up for *sale,*
but frankly and obviously
they really didn't give a *care.*

These weren't animals, ivory,
tools or even *gold.*
These were people . . . real people . . .
intellectual people they *sold.*

Up for sale were architects
and *mathematicians,*
mechanics, entertainers, singers,
and yes, *politicians,*
dancers, philosophers,
specialists in *irrigation,*
theologians, doctors,
teachers full of *information,*
astronomers, lawyers, skilled miners,
and *scientists,*
soldiers, writers, engineers,
not to mention *artists,*
adventurers, farmers, herders,
and devout *'Kings',*
comedians, judges, professors,
and mighty *'Queens'.*

In Africa,

these accomplishments had already been *achieved.*

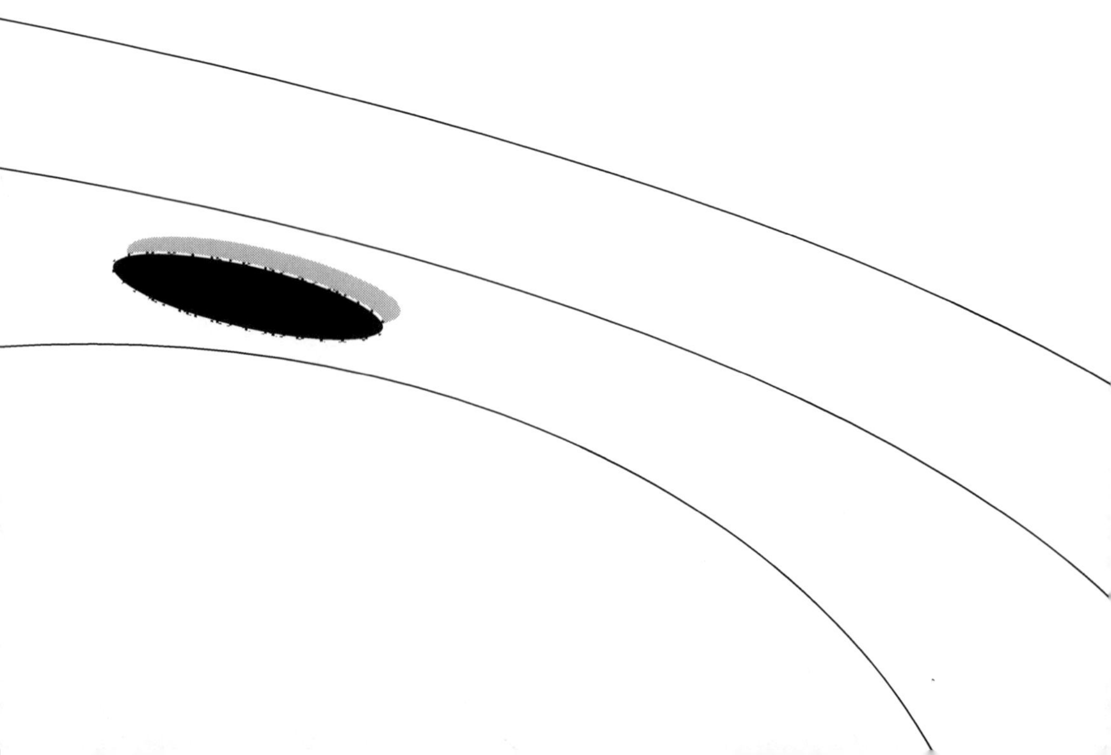

Europeans were deceived
not to treat Africans as GREAT as *these.*

Oh,

the things they had to endure

in this sad, but true *story*.

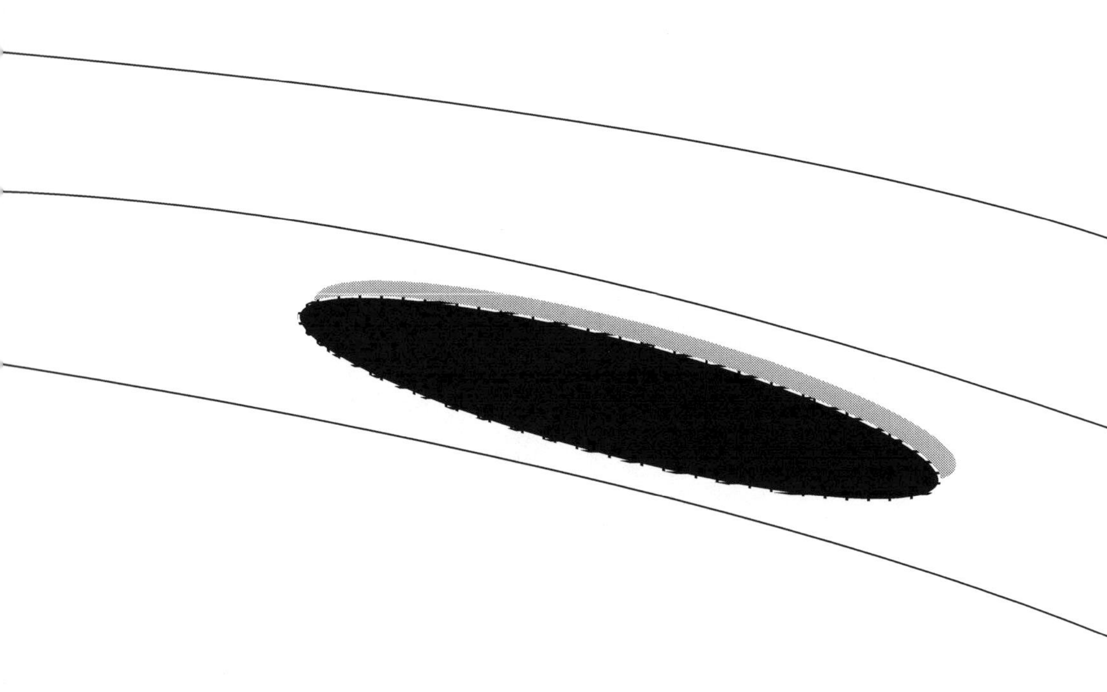

Although abused and misused,
the "black race" is still
destined for *glory!*

Hurdle #2

Enslavement

Just like going to the market
to pick up bread and *butter,*
auction day for slave masters
was just like none *other.*

They had been so desensitized
to the highest *degree.*
Despite what they "see" ,
they chose not to see slaves *humanity.*

Inspected and examined
just as a jockey would a *horse,*
the white man would probe and poke
and prod slaves with *force.*

They would shave their heads
and **strip them** of their *clothes*
and then brand them with hot metal
to claim who they now *"own"*.

Here again we see wives and husbands
separated from each *other,*
children taken away from siblings,
fathers and grieving *mothers,*
since plantation owners wanted
one family member and not *another,*
the black family again has been split apart.

How can they *recover?*

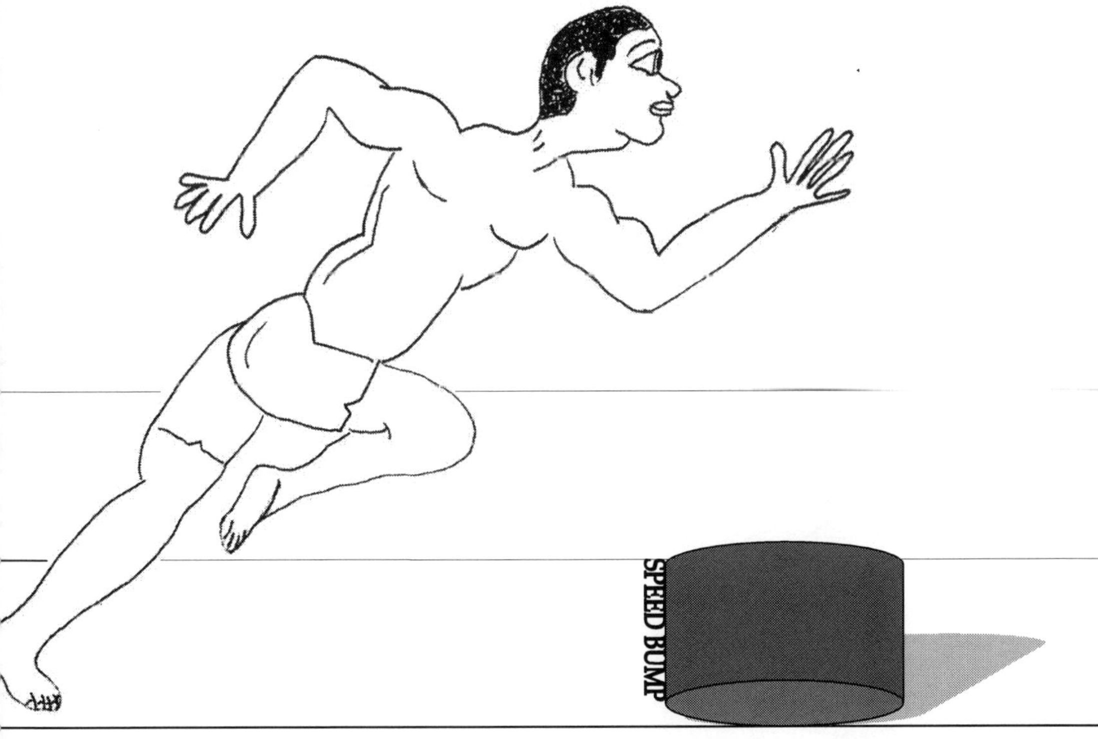

No longer allowed to keep their birth name
representing African *pride,*
slave masters changed slaves names
and expected when called, for them to *reply.*

These white men used a strategic system
to conquer and *divide*
by creating friction between field slaves
and domestic slaves working *inside.*

Field slaves labored hard on plantations
and were typically darker-*skinned.*
House slaves' labor was slightly better
and their lighter-skin often got them *in.*

Slaveholders even forced a slave driver
that was none other but their *own,*
- just another black man -
forced to whip his own people
when he was *told.*

This was all done maliciously
and all done by *design,*
to cause envy, hostility
and tension all on the front *line*
because slave masters knowingly realized
and were clearly *aware,*
to keep slaves under control
they must cause severe dissension and *fear.*

Despite the fear overflowing
in the minds of many of these *slaves,*
the pain was too much to bear,
so some chose to GET OUT and run *away!*

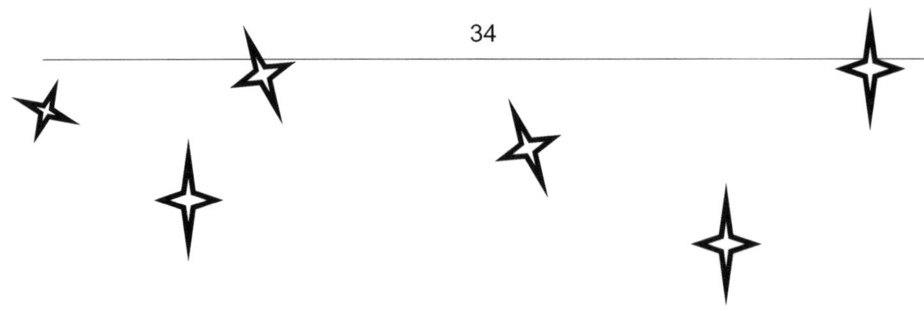

Many were successful as they fled
the treacherous journey to the *North,*
as they used the **Underground Railroad**,
with hopes of freedom to come *forth!*

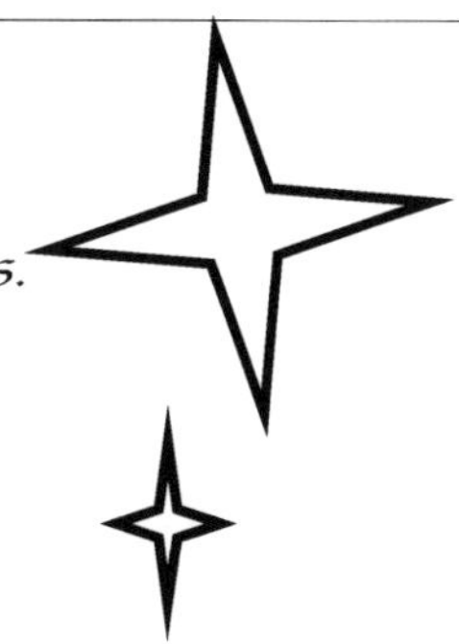

The Underground Railroad
was not a track for any subways or *trains.*
It was a pathway to the North
for desperate running slaves to *escape.*

Secret routes and safe houses
were all kept in hidden *codes,*
as abolitionists - both black and white-
assisted these slaves to their new homes.

Ways of escaping slavery
took ingenious courage that is *great.*
And one of the most interesting escapes
is **Henry 'Box' Brown** shipped in a *crate.*

Henry was a slave in Richmond, Virginia
and he was hit with extreme *heartbreak*
when his wife and kids were sold away.
Helpless . . . their chains he couldn't *break.*

So he decided enough is enough
and fit himself inside a *crate,*
to be shipped in a box for 27 hours
to Philadelphia to *liberate!*

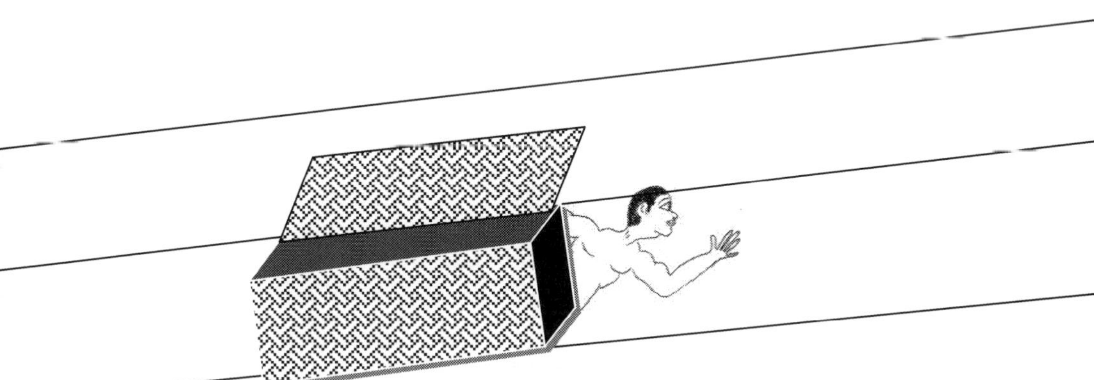

Other slaves chose to rebel,
rising in opposition to *slaveholders.*
And one of the largest slave revolts
was led by none other than ***Nat Turner.***

In Virginia
and in the year of *1831,*
he believed he was divinely chosen
and then he saw a sign from the strange *sun.*

He wanted to avenge slavery,
so he gathered up a team of strong *slaves*
to fight for the cause of freedom
and against depraved ways whites behaved.

He was an educated slave.
He knew the bible inside and *out.*
A man of faith. He trusted in God
and knew uprisings marked a dangerous *route.*

Now, 1861
through *1865*
was the bloodiest war in America :
Over half a million soldiers *died.*

The American Civil War
- a battle between the North and *South* -
gave hope of preserving the Union,
so slavery in the Confederacy is no longer *allowed.*

Refusing to grant freedom
to who they say is rightfully *theirs,*
slave owners ignored the President's orders
to free slaves from their *despair.*

However in 1865,
with the surrender from the *Confederacy,*
news spread that slavery was abolished . . .
but some slaves weren't told they were *free.*

Oh,

the things they had to endure

in this sad, but true *story*.

Although abused and misused,
the "black race" is still
destined for *glory!*

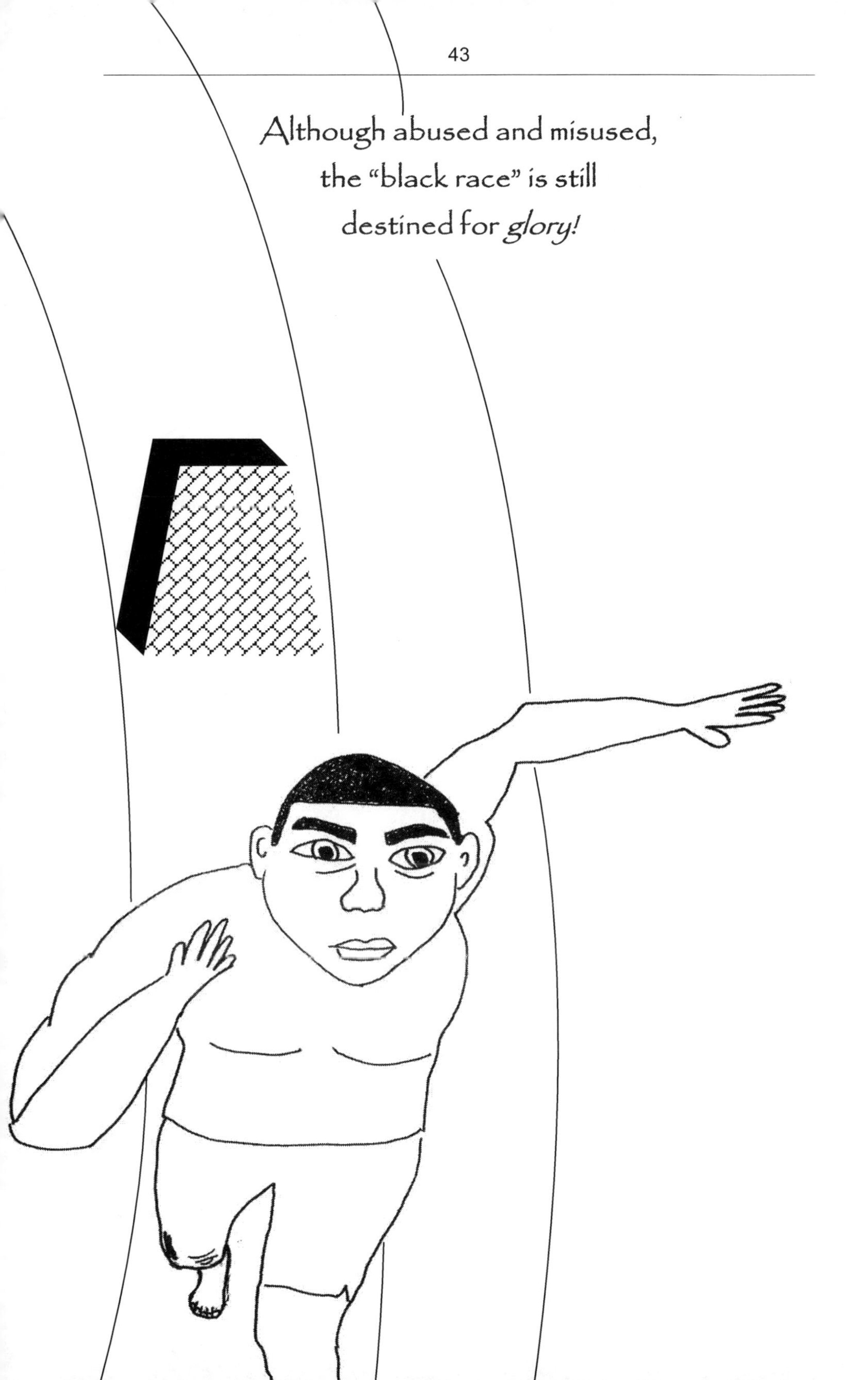

Hurdle #3

Reconstruction Era

When the enslaved were finally set free,
a joyous celebration was *due,*
but as they walked away from slavery,
they had nowhere else to turn *to.*

With no property, land, food,
resources or much-needed *support . . .*
black people, again,
had to be creative
to survive and thrive as a *resort.*

Fast forward to years ahead,
blacks were still fighting a battle *uphill.*
Not able to read or write,
blacks were lacking a job's pertinent *skills.*

Their freedom did not mean equal rights
or respect for their new *start* . . .

because the **'changing of the laws'**
does not mean **'changing of the *heart*'**.

Racism and discrimination
ran rampant throughout the *nation,*
as many whites still felt that blacks
were an inferior *creation.*

This period (a time meant for
positivity and ***'Reconstruction'****)*
was actually - for many blacks -
a time for bad and moral *corruption.*

Black men were often jailed
for small offenses or none at *all,*
putting them back in enslavement,
made legal in the 13th Amendment *law.*

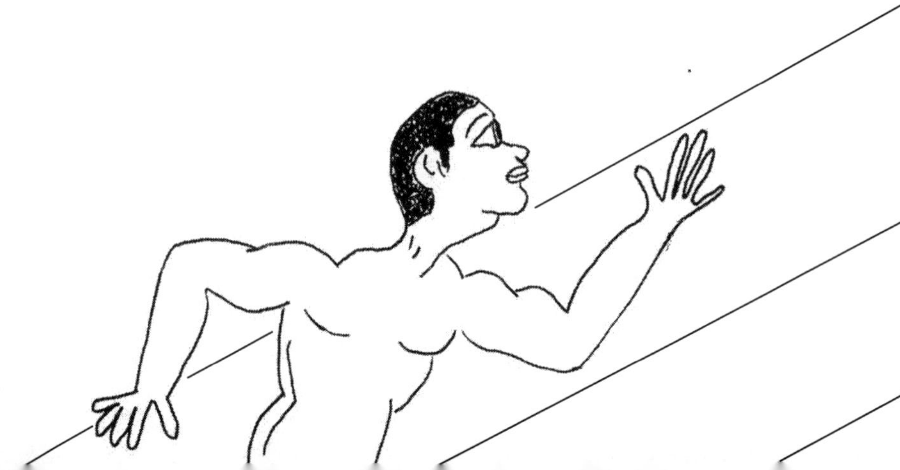

The increase of black convicts
did a great number of *things.*
It criminalized black people
and launched harsh ***convict leasing.***

The imprisonment of countless blacks
pushed and added to the *narrative*
that they were villains and wrongdoers
and that freeing slaves was a *negative.*

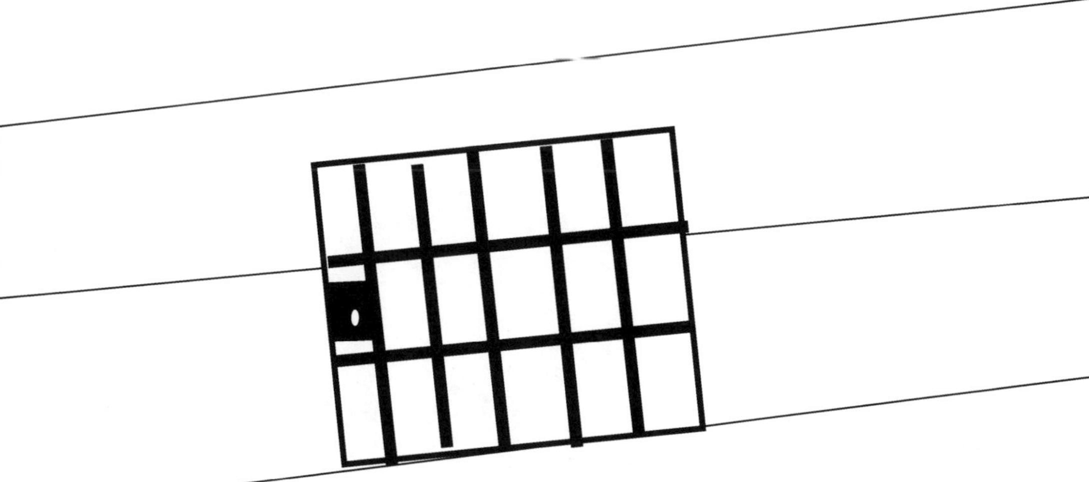

Black codes were laws created to ensure blacks had lesser rights than *whites*.

Jim Crow laws enforced segregation by race and unequal human *rights*.

Drinking water fountains, restaurants,
        and even *restrooms*,
public places, public transportation,
        and also public *schools*
were all separated and unfairly financed
        by the color of their *skin*.
This 'separate but equal' deal
        was obviously a one-sided *win!*

Oh,

the things they had to endure

in this sad, but true *story*.

Although abused and misused,
the "black race" is still
destined for *glory!*

Hurdle #4

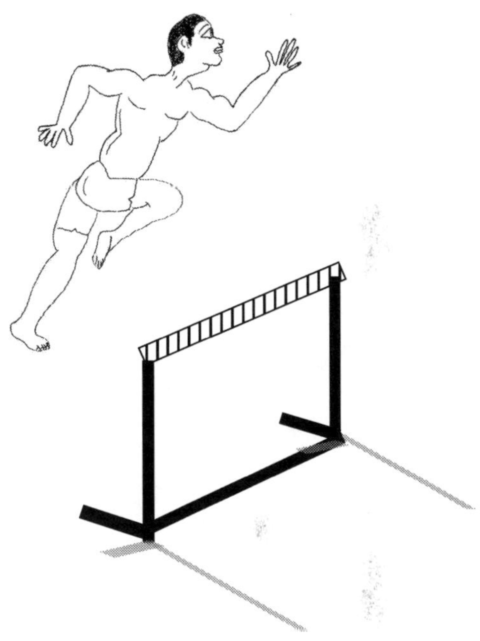

Bigotry

(racism, prejudice, intolerance)

You may or may not have heard of
Tulsa, Oklahoma's ***"Black Wall Street"***.
It was a booming and thriving community
where affluent blacks lived a glorious *feat.*

With movie theaters, luxury shops,
a library and lovely *hotels*...
lawyers, doctors, and dentists
and other black businesses that *excelled.*
Blacks were supporting one another.
They kept their money spent within.
But on May 31st, 1921,
this all came to a horrific end.

A white mob devastated this neighborhood.
They were outraged by alleged *news:*
A black shoe shiner assaulted a white lady,
but there's no confirmation this is *true.*

Black men came to support this young man.
Whites came to take this young man's *life.*
And this perpetuated to a massacre,
killing hundreds of innocent black *lives.*

Thousands of whites armed and dangerous
happy to destroy what blacks optimized,
attacked residents,
destroyed homes,
burned buildings and
used planes to shower
bullets from the *sky.*

To add insult to injury,
discrimination was alive on film and on *stage*,
as white people used their platform
to make blacks look brainless and *strange*.

White minstrel performers would paint
their complete, entire face with black *paint*.
Around their mouth they'd paint with white,
like a clown with totally no *restraint*.

They would entertain an audience
with a so-called art form . . .
known as ***blackface,***
to portray black people
as buffoons and idiots
falsely representing the entire *race*.

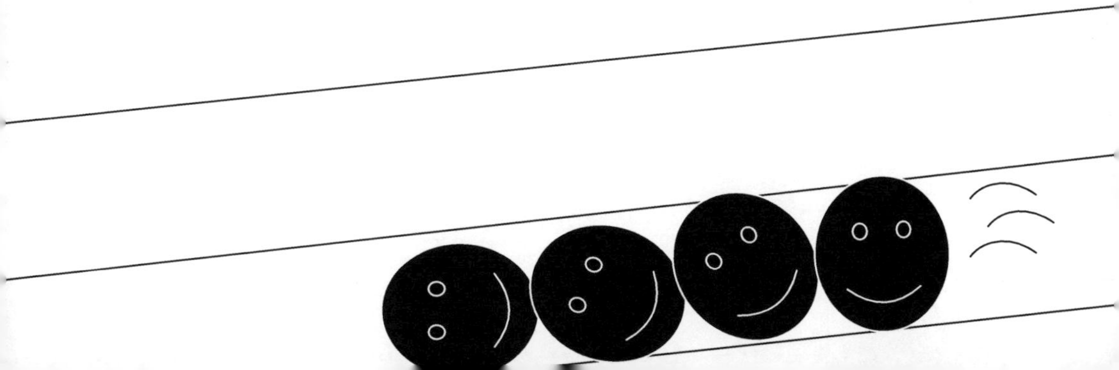

Even if a black person wanted to travel,
they couldn't
and shouldn't
leave home *without*
the travel guide called the Green Book
for trips
and journeys
and cruising *about.*

This book listed all the establishments
that were safe and friendly for blacks to *eat,*
places to visit . . . routes to avoid . . .
hotels where they were welcome to *sleep.*

It's so sad and unfortunate
this book was ever needed to be *conceived.*
But it helped to save many black people
from potential confrontation and *injury.*

Blacks wouldn't dare let the sun set
while traveling in the wrong town's *grounds.*
They used the **Green Book** to navigate
far away from **Sundown Towns**.

For 'driving while black'
in these neighborhoods
was sure to give blacks a beat *down,*
since **Jim Crow** laws were strictly enforced
and racial segregation was rampant *around.*

It is one thing to have people in multitudes
literally detest you in your *face*.
Even worse are government programs
against your best interest put into *place*.

The government gave money for slavery,
but <u>NOT</u> one dime went to any *slaves*.
About 300 dollars per slave was given
to slaveholders as *loss of property* to *aid*.

Also,
workers in agriculture
and servants that worked *domestically*
were banned from receiving
retirement income,
although fully *deserving.*

Low income workers made little money
and unable to save for *retirement,*
just another way blacks were shunned
and pushed aside from the *government.*

So as workers aged and got older,
unable to keep their inabilities *hidden,*
they now relied on the income
and finances of their hardworking *children.*

If you didn't know already,
owning property is the way to *wealth,*
but this form of getting ahead for blacks,
went absolutely *stealth.*

Whites were able to pass down their assets
from generation to *generation,*
since their home ownership gave them
home equity and home *appreciation.*

Redlining was one way (out of many)
to prevent blacks from getting *ahead,*
as it denied blacks a home loan,
while the dream of home ownership *spread.*

Only certain neighborhoods . . .
for certain *people* . . .

with a certain income . . .
(proving there's no "separate but *equal*"),

qualified for this
government sanctioned practice,

intended for segregation,
and in some places . . . still in *action.*

Oh,

the things they had to endure

in this sad, but true *story*.

Although abused and misused,
the "black race" is still
destined for *glory!*

Hurdle #5

Integration

(Civil Rights Movement)

The 1950s and 1960s
was the Civil Rights *Movement,*
where blacks fought for equal rights
and social justice *improvements.*

The hate was strong, the hate was real,
the hate saturated the *towns.*
Whites may have feared they'd lose power
to blacks slowly gaining *ground.*

In 1954
was Brown versus Board of *Education.*
Its purpose was to eliminate
public schools from racial *segregation.*
Those in the south decided to go
against the Supreme Court's *decision*
and keep their schools just like they were -
with no blacks in clear view *vision.*

In 1957,
on their first day of *school,*
black high school students were met
with nothing but rude and *cruel.*

The Little Rock Nine
(these nine students are best known *as*)
were not allowed to enter the school
that was all white until *now.*

Disappointed,
these students came up against a *"wall"*
of National Guards sent by
the Governor of *Arkansas.*

They blocked these nine students
from entering *inside*,
since the idea of integration
caused many to be *mortified*.

With constant verbal and emotional
and physical *attacks*,
these nine showed courage, stuck together
and had each other's *back*.

In 1960,
the first black child in the *south*
went to school - completely white -
now that <u>integration</u> *allows*.

Protected by U.S. Marshals
-walking 6-years old and *proud*-
she was guarded from violent threats
yelled from angry protesting *crowds*.

Only one white teacher was brave,
bold and courageous enough to *stay*
to teach little **Ruby Bridges** when
other teachers refused and went *away*.

Also, a series of young people,
both black and *white,*
arranged **sit-in demonstrations**
for the movement of civil *rights.*

They would sit at lunch counters,
that declined to serve *blacks,*
however all they got in return
was ridicule, scorn and *attack.*

Retaliation from whites
came in many *forms:*
Vinegar, coffee, ketchup, sugar . . .
on their heads, they were *poured.*

Fists were swung, bodies thrown
and of course the media was *lured*
while photos and videos spread all around.
The nation watched and it struck a *chord.*

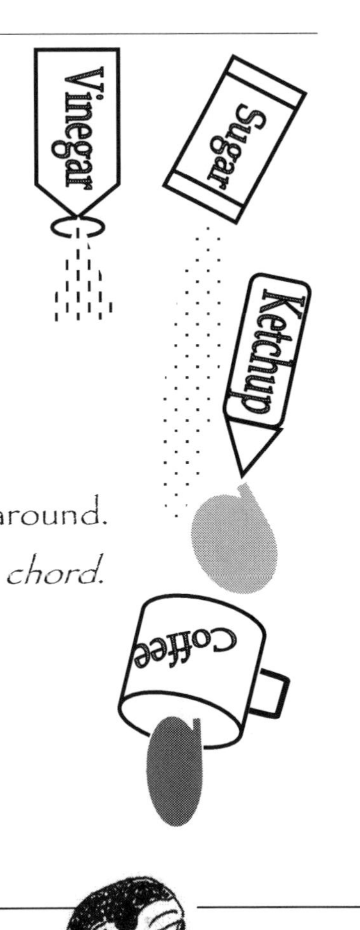

In an effort for social change,
young and old and mixed racial *groups*
joined together to ride buses
in the deep south . . . but met *disputes.*

These **Freedom Riders** were audacious
to challenge segregated local *laws,*
as they were arrested and assaulted,
buses burned and knowing some will *fall.*

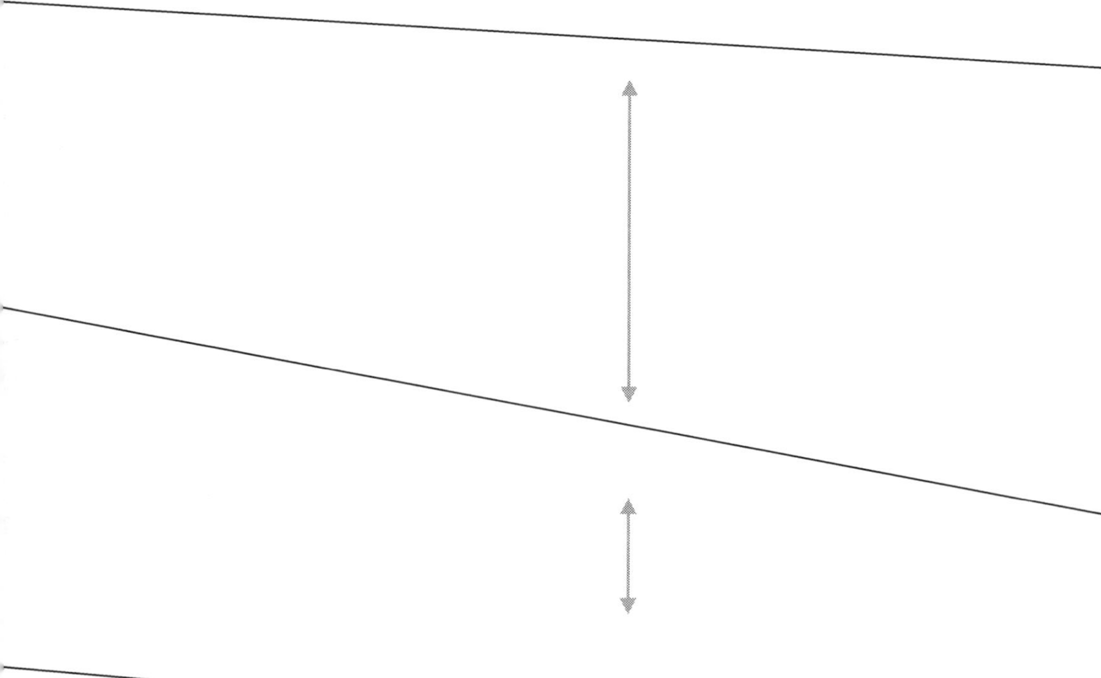

They helped to spotlight the oppression blacks endured, especially in the *south*. Their non-violent and peaceful disposition had a lasting impression to those all *around*.

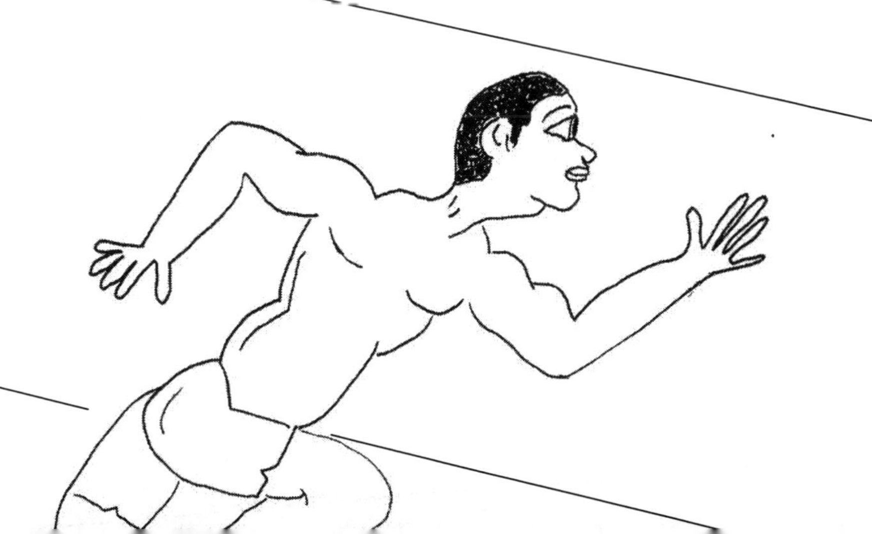

Oh,

the things they had to endure

in this sad, but true *story*.

Although abused and misused,
the "black race" is still
destined for *glory!*

Hurdle #6

Activists' Plight

(During the Civil Rights Movement)

One day in **1955**,
a civil rights *activist*,
refused to give up her seat.
They said get up. She didn't submit..

Rosa Parks wasn't getting up for no one
and not even for a white *man*.
She knew she had just as much of a right
to sit on that bus since she's a *human*.

Soon arrested for violating
the unfair segregation *laws*,
this event united black people
igniting a bus boycott for the *cause*.

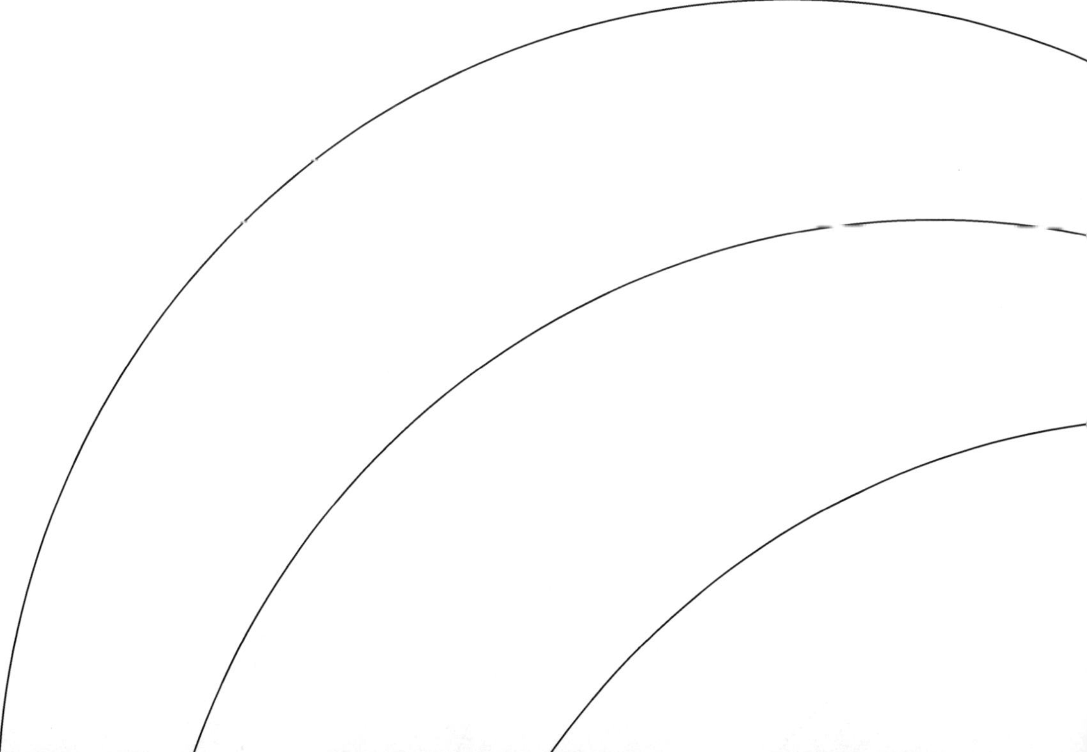

Blacks sought other means for transit.
They just would not ride the *bus*.
They had to endure and persevere
during *The Montgomery Bus Boycott.*

They would walk, or carpool
or take a taxi with black *drivers*.
They would do all they could,
sticking together until justice *transpired*.

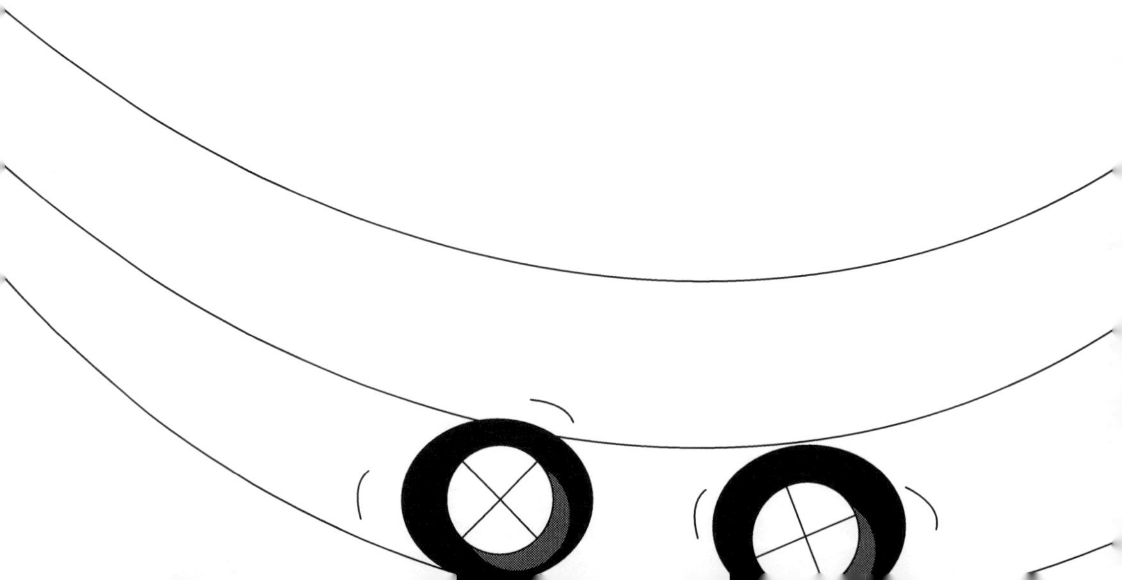

Lasting over an entire year,
this protest was *groundbreaking.*
Black leadership emerged with help from
Dr. Martin Luther King's *undertaking.*

Finding it unconstitutional,
the Supreme Court decided,
that segregation on buses
shall be no more . . . no longer *invited.*

Dr. Martin Luther King
rose up to national *prominence*
and is best known for his contribution
towards civil rights with *non-violence*.

He was a Pastor and a Leader
and a Husband and a *Dad,*
initiating peaceful marches
and speeches on societies *'bads'*. . .
like the discriminatory practices
still preventing blacks to *vote:*

Blacks were forced to pay poll taxes,
discouraging voting as they'd *hoped.*
To get blacks to turn away,
they were given hard literacy *tests,*
and they were beaten
and intimidated with mad and angry *threats.*

Dr. Martin Luther King
and so, so many others strived
and were successful at helping
The Voting Rights of 1965.
However, on April 4th ... in 1968,
he was assassinated and died.
"I Have a Dream" still lives strong today.

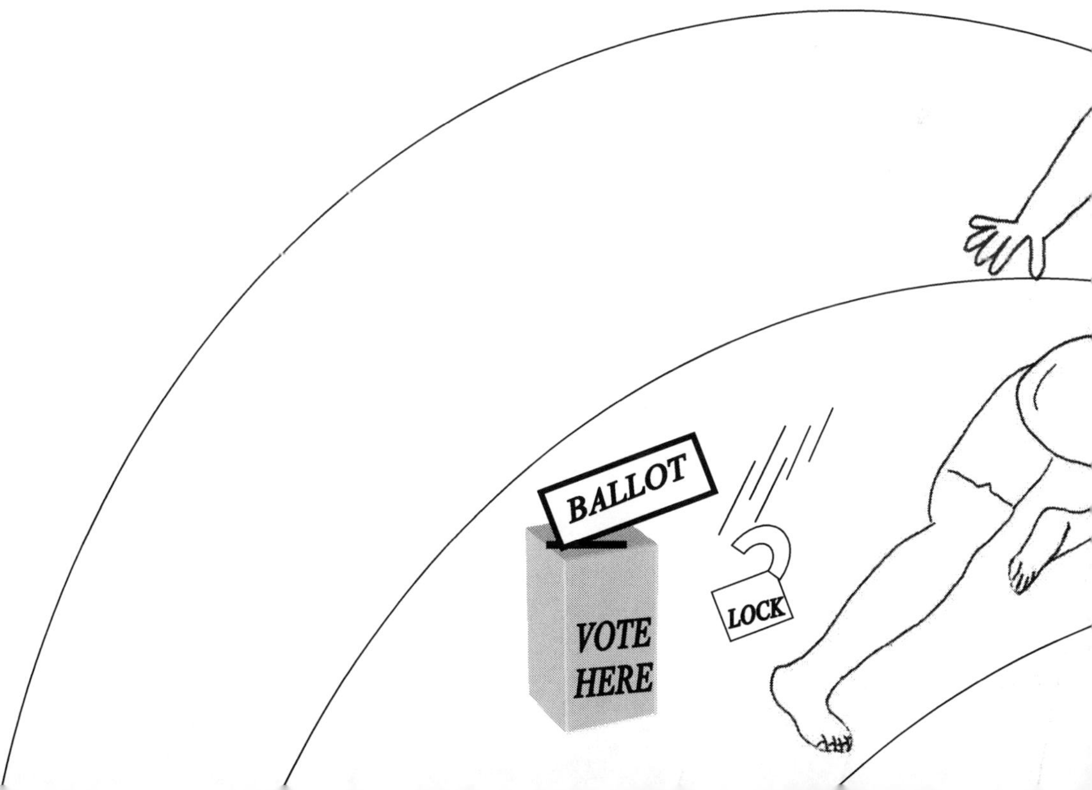

A very articulate **Malcolm X**
-a black human rights *activist*-
strongly influenced many blacks
to know their true value as they *exist*.

He urged blacks to defend themselves
"by any means *necessary*",
as he passionately pushed for
the rights of blacks with his *commentary*.

Blacks were being attacked
by the very persons hired to *protect*
citizens in the community -
but blacks received little to no *respect*.

During peaceful protests
police would bring out their snarling *dogs.*
Firemen would point high pressure hoses
at blacks and spray water out in *gobs.*

Because of this type of behavior,
Malcolm X was determined more than *ever,*
to make sure fellow brothers and sisters
were empowered and educated *better.*

However,
on February 21st in 1965,
Malcolm X was speaking at a rally.
He was assassinated and died.

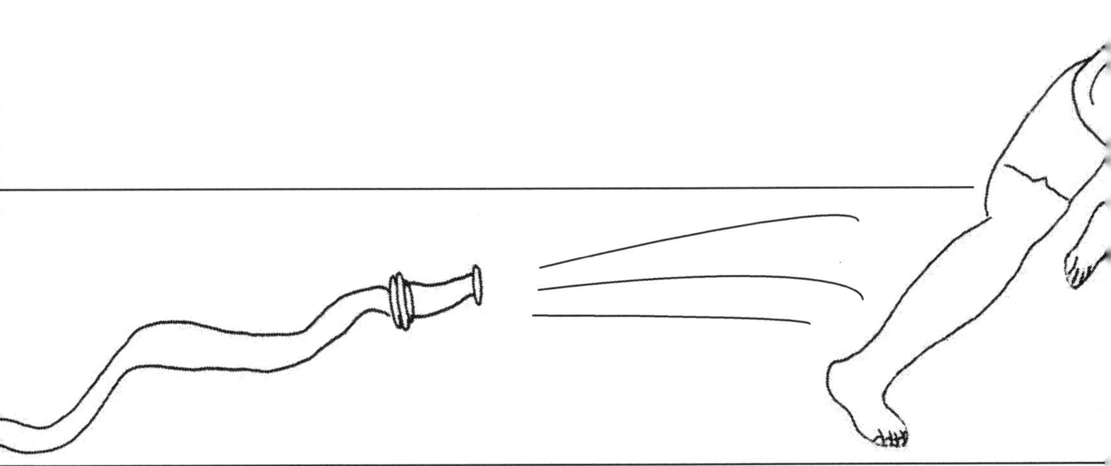

In **1964**,
a Florida *hotel*...
only served and offered service
to other white *clientele*.

Black and white activists
had a plan to *promote*,
so they jumped in the swimming pool
against hotel policies to *revolt*.

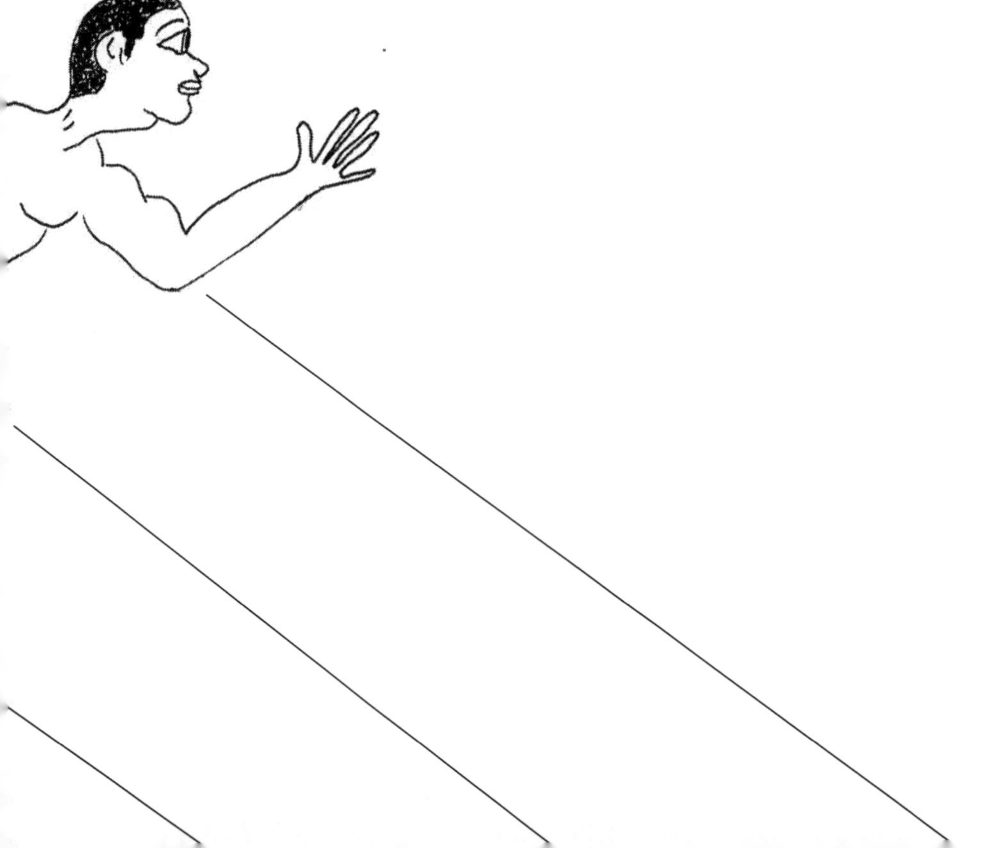

The hotel manager responded
with complete *harshness*
by dumping acid into the pool
to push out the *activists.*

This protest helped push
the **Civil Rights Act** into *effect.*
Without sacrifices of people like these
segregation would still *exist.*

At a time when men . . .

were being drafted to *fight* . . .

in the Vietnam War . . .

black men and women would *unite.*

In 1966,
Black Panthers plan *pioneered.*
They said, "If we're going to put up a fight,
then we need to fight our battles right *here."*

In their black leather jackets
their image was *uniform.*
Their black berets adorned their heads,
while holding their weapons that yelled REFORM!!!!

They wanted freedom for black people,
full employment
and a decent *house* . . .
education teaching black- pride,
release for black prisoners
in the *jailhouse*.
They wanted black men exempt from military.
They wanted justice.
They wanted *peace*.
They wanted the end to senseless murders
and to stop police *brutality*.

To protest and bring exposure
to the wrongs being done to *blacks,*
two bold men used their huge platform,
but in response, received much *flak.*

Tommie Smith and **John Carlos**
were sprinters running
for the *United States.*
During the Olympics with many viewers,
they made a risky,
yet courageous *case.*

They won a Gold and Bronze medal,
earning their right
to stand on the *platform*
and as they walked carrying their shoes,
they walked in socks
protesting for the *poor.*

Beads and a black scarf around their neck
protested the revolting lynching of *blacks.*
Their black- gloved fists raised in the air
became a Black Power civil rights *act!*

Seeking for social equality
cost these young men a lot of *distress.*
They lost their jobs, received death threats
and never again allowed to run for the *U.S.*

If you think about these highlighted years,
they aren't too much far *behind.*
All these events happened fairly recent . . .
not in long ago ancient *times.*

America is not too much removed
from slavery or the *Civil Rights Movement.*
There's been many gains,
yet many setbacks,
to social justice *improvements.*

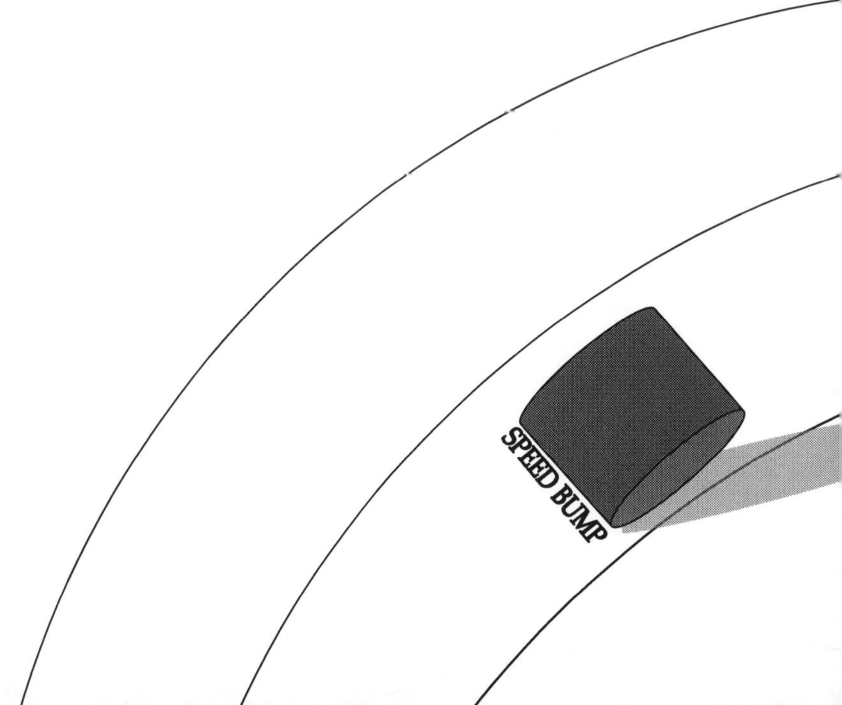

Oh,

the things they had to endure

in this sad, but true *story*.

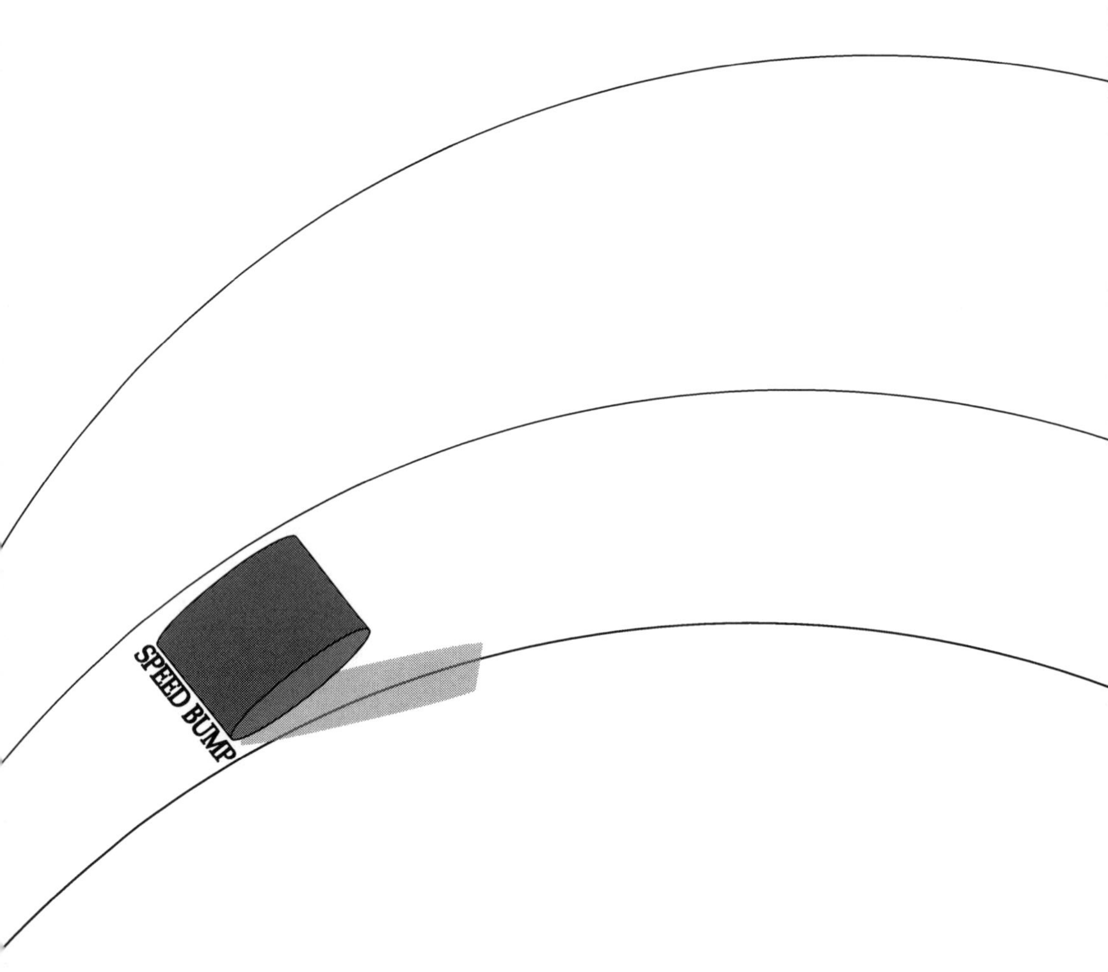

Although abused and misused,
the "black race" is still
destined for *glory!*

Hurdle #7

Breaking Down Stereotypes

The policy Affirmative Action
-for employment and *education*-
was meant to level the playing field,
for those hurt by previous *discrimination*.

As they began putting forth the effort
-these Colleges and *Universities*-
attempted to improve admissions process
with justice and *equity*.

Not just for blacks, but everyone
would benefit from *diversity.*

Not just for blacks, but everyone
would benefit *interpersonally.*

Prejudices and <u>stereotypes</u>
was believed to be *reduced,*
as everyone from every which where,
got to know and learn each other's *truth.*

Minorities, such as blacks,
had more access to higher *education,*
however many banned this new policy
saying it's reverse *discrimination.*

You see, everybody is in a race
no matter what era they live *in,*
whether it's the race to end slavery
or if it's the race for segregation to *end.*

It might be the race for equal education,
fair employment and peace of *mind.*
Or the race just to be treated as human
and running without seeing the finish *line.*

Everybody is in a race
and everyone should have a fair *shot,*
void of **certain** obstacles in their lane
intended to get **certain** runners to *stop.*

No matter what your race is
with all the atrocities you may *face,*
keep moving,
keep strutting in the right direction.
Continue to run your *race!*

Like **Frederick Douglas** you might
not really want to smile in *photographs*
because you want to make a point
that injustice doesn't bring smiles or *laughs.*

Unlike social media today
where people post their life
that may be *fraud*
- phony laughing and being fake happy-
his image made a powerful point
that is *strong.*

As a runaway slave . . .
turned prominent *activist* . . .
turned author . . . turned speaker,
and leader in the rise of *abolitionists,*
Frederick Douglas was the most photographed
in the 19th *century.*
It was his intention to show the world
the face of a black man that is *free.*

Against the many stereotypes,
like the images of "happy *slaves*",
his photos show true humanity and
opposed ways blacks had been *displayed.*

So, like the **Tuskegee Airmen**
you may be **un**appreciated and **under**rated.
With honor they served their country
through much adversity often advocated.

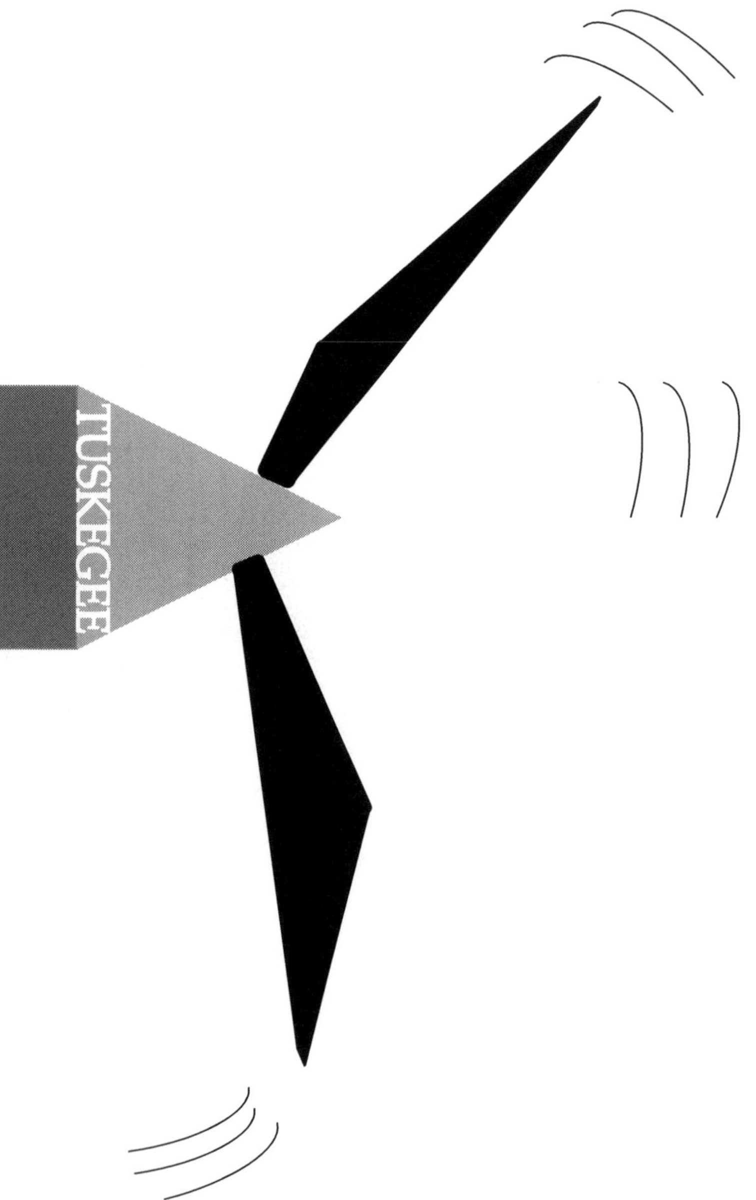

They proved they were more
than capable to fly
their red-tailed painted *planes*
and when faced with hate
towards their black skin,
their perseverance always *remained*.

You may feel like a **Buffalo Soldier.**
They carried a banner and a *flag*
without fully being able to live out
the liberty it promises they should *have.*

Formed in **1866**,
the African American *Regiments,*
are best known for their valiant fighting
and helping Westward Expansion *Settlements.*

Discriminated and thought to be incapable,
given the worst equipment the army *had,*
Buffalo Soldiers still gave their best,
fighting for more than just fellow *comrades.*

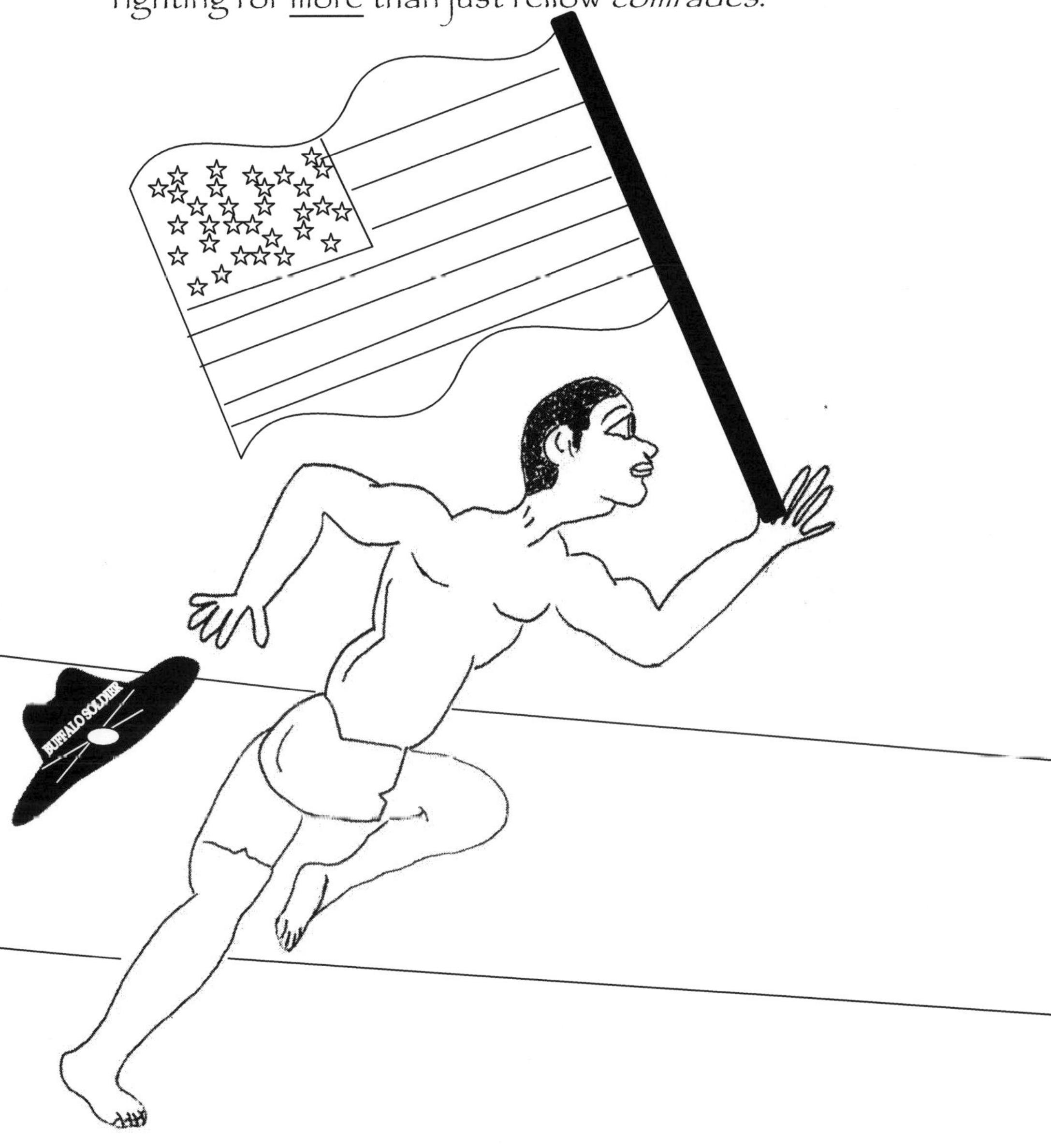

Oh,
the things they had to endure
in this sad, but true *story*.

Although abused and misused,
the "black race" is still
destined for *glory!*

Hurdle #8

The Impact of Slavery on Modern America

You'll see your Oprahs and Obamas,
Michael Jordans and *Jay Z's.*
You'll see your real estate moguls,
black business owners . . . blacks on *tv.*

These are your black elite . . . the rich,
they've earned success and great *wealth.*
But this doesn't represent
the entire black race as a whole within *itself.*

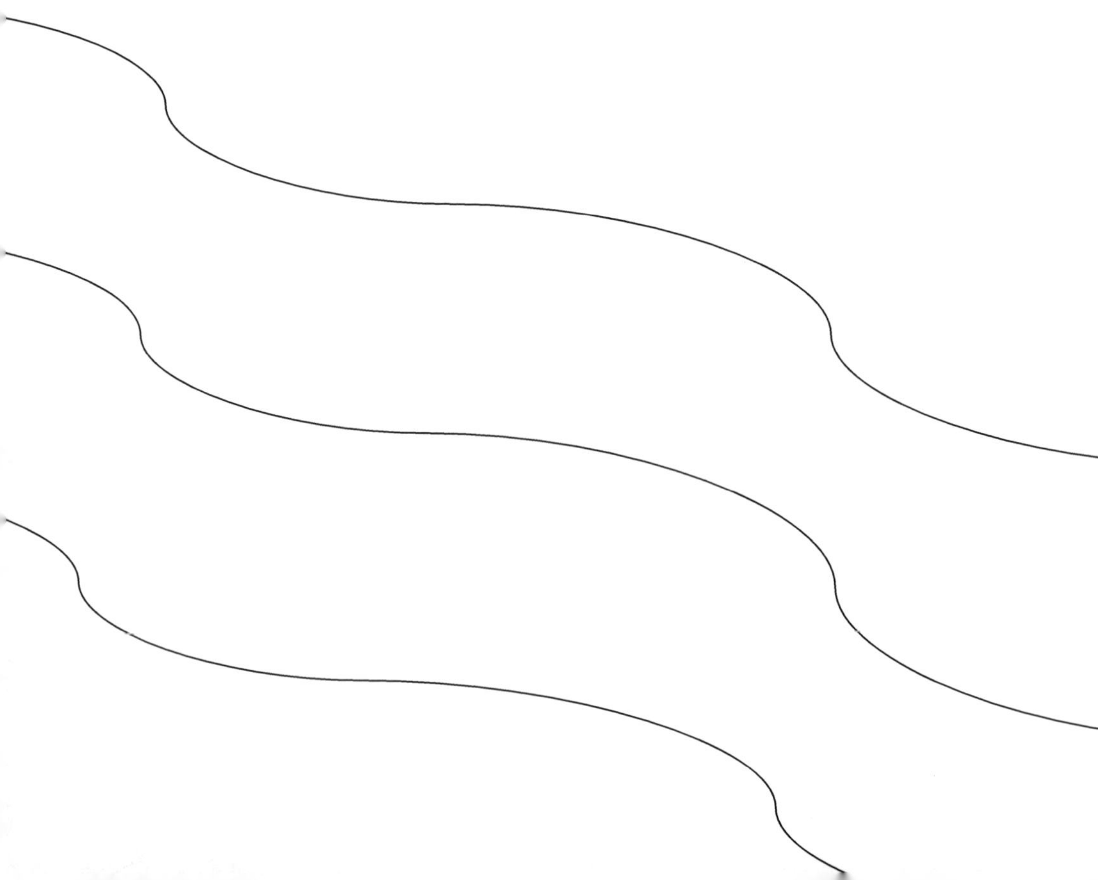

Out of millions of black folks,
this wealth is like a grain of sand on the *beach*.
It's just a drop in a bucket,
comparing black elite to blacks in poverty's *reach*.

So, there is still a **systemic problem**
that blacks still languish in poverty *today*.
Until Americans become more conscious,
our current state of poverty will never *change*.

Hence, there were many families
in need of financial *assistance,*
so AFDC provided **welfare**
from 1935 through *1996.*

This Aid to Families with Dependent Children
was first designed for white single *mothers*
that qualified if their man were deceased , absent,
or there was an unemployed *father.*

Later extended to black women,
the rules coincidentally *changed,*
mandating the no " man in the house" rule
and if a man was found . . . they'll get no more *aid.*

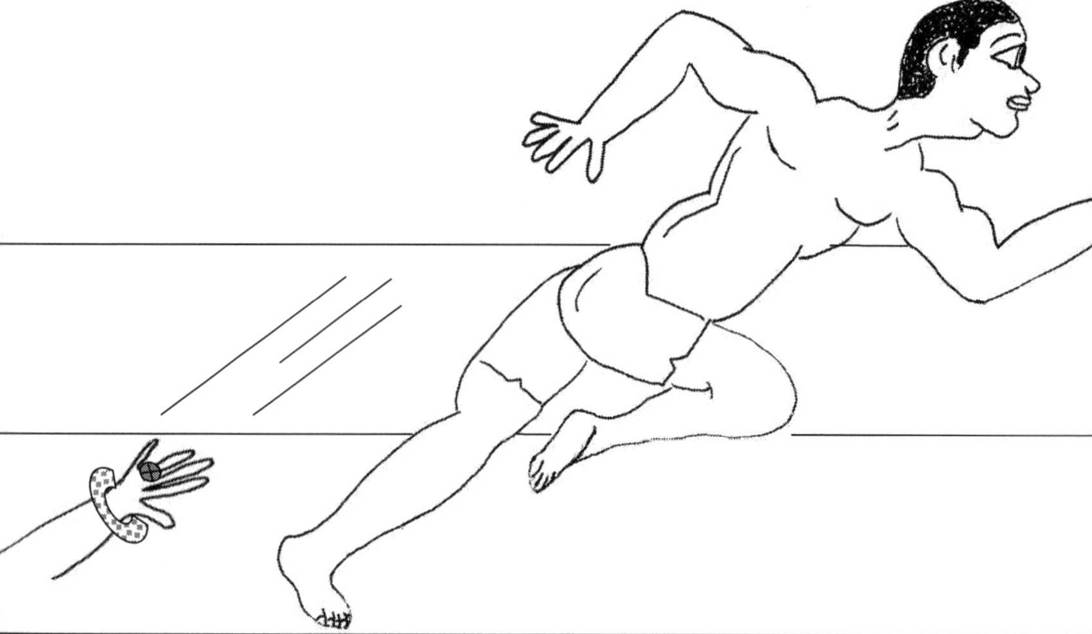

The government's
no " man in the house" rule
seemed to endorse spouses to *divorce,*
women to not marry,
encouraged more child-bearing,
reminiscent to how slaves were
separated by *force.*

This government social policy,
caused many families to be *dependent,*
with little incentive for a two-parent household,
and a cycle of poverty apparently *intended.*

The disparities between blacks and whites
are still alive and well *today,*
with how some schools respond to students
with similar behaviors they *convey.*

Stereotypes that certain boys are "bad"
and other boys are "studious
and just likes to *play"*
is evident with how some schools
respond to black and white students
in different *ways.*

A psychologist will assess a child
to see if they're in need
of **special *education,***
but unfortunately too many black boys
are suggested
under this *classification.*

Separated from the general population,
given remedial
and watered-down *curriculum,*
black boys fill up these special ed classes
and are the most likely
to be labeled in *sum.*

Black boys are also least likely
to be classified as 'gifted or *talented',*
even if their test scores and performance
prove they are more than *adequate.*

As seen before in past years,
this is truly nothing *new.*
Black children are harshly labeled
for behavior other races clearly *do.*

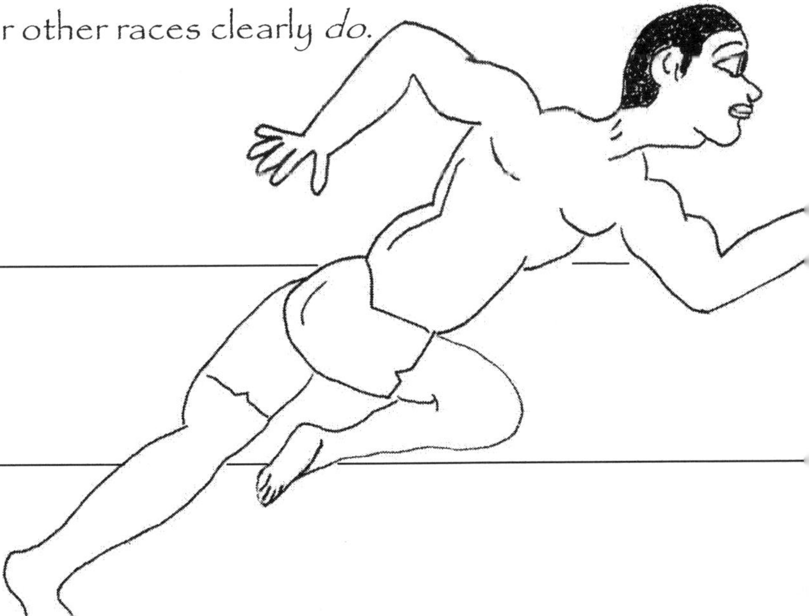

This disparity doesn't stop here.
It continues down the pipeline to **jails**,
Poor black men are the largest percentage
to be incarcerated at a large *scale*.

Like the origin of the **War on Drugs**
had a purpose that
unfairly sentenced *blacks*.
Some in the white community
were doing cocaine,
while the black community
was introduced to *crack*.

If caught with drugs by the authorities
(these two drugs were essentially the *same)*,
white people were treated
as addicts needing help,
while blacks were treated
as criminals to *blame*.

Blacks were sentenced longer in prison,
and made to be second-class *citizens*
and after they served their time in jail
they struggled in the society they lived *in.*

Even as a non-violent offender,
they're now discriminated and *excluded.*
Going to school or getting a job
is nearly impossible . . . research has *concluded.*

Labeled and branded as a criminal,
history seemed to have repeat *itself,*
similar to Jim Crow Laws
that were obvious,
this system keeps <u>legal discrimination</u> in *effect.*

The senseless killings of unarmed blacks
made **police** create
a BRAND for *themselves.*
When black people get pulled over,
they think they're about
to take their last *breathe.*

Just hearing the sirens ring
from black and blue cops meant to *protect,*
causes fear that they may see them
- an innocent civilian - as a living *threat.*

One too many times during slavery,
authorities seldom had a slave's *back.*

One too many times during protests,
authorities <u>used batons</u> to *attack blacks.*

Many cops are good, but some are bad-
creating distrust in the black *community.*
Blacks still hope ***the good ones*** help
to put an end to racial profiling they see.

Bad policing has created a BRAND,
it doesn't matter if the cop is black or *white,*
just the mere fact that they are an officer
trigger detests in some blacks *eyesight.*

And the anger will only continue to grow,
when crooked cops continue to go *free*
and repeat . . . and repeat . . . and repeat,
the black experience in *history.*

And just as slave masters would pick a slave
to beat and punish and whip his *own,*
Music producers have done the same,
with destructive music
bumping through *earphones.*

This music destroys the black community
and creates a bad image for many *blacks.*
As those in power intentionally
push this profane narrative
of *blacks as facts.*

They'll find a musician that's excited
and eager and hungry for *"success"*,
that'll say just about anything
representing blacks with a negative *mindset.*

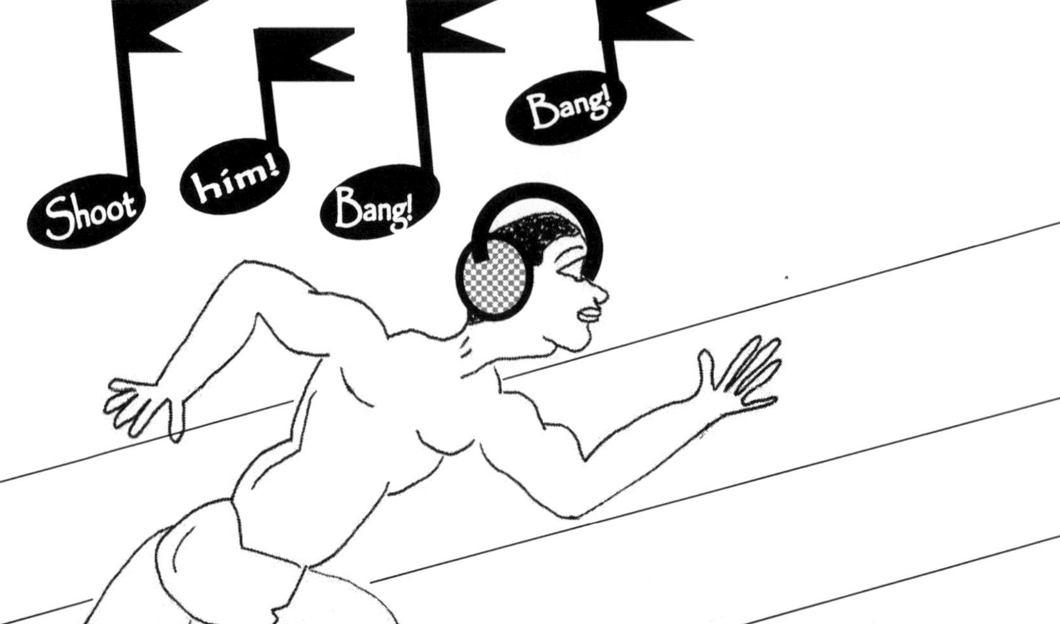

"Shoot him . . . disrespect her,
bang bang . . . drugs galore,
N-word this . . . N- word that,
look at me . . .
I'm a scary cat!"

Instead of reciting
their poetry of the streets
by using their awesome gifts to *enlighten,*
some send a message to everyone
blacks are uncivilized . . .
YET interests are *heightened.*

Oh,
the things they had to endure
in this sad, but true *story*.

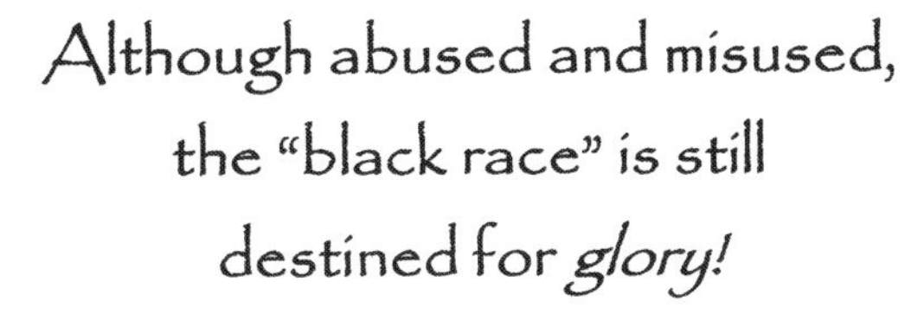
Although abused and misused,
the "black race" is still
destined for *glory!*

Racism still exists,
but it may not look like it once did *before.*

There may no longer be slavery,
but convict leasing
echoed that past even *more*.

There may no longer be Jim Crow Laws,
but mass incarceration has the same *effect*.

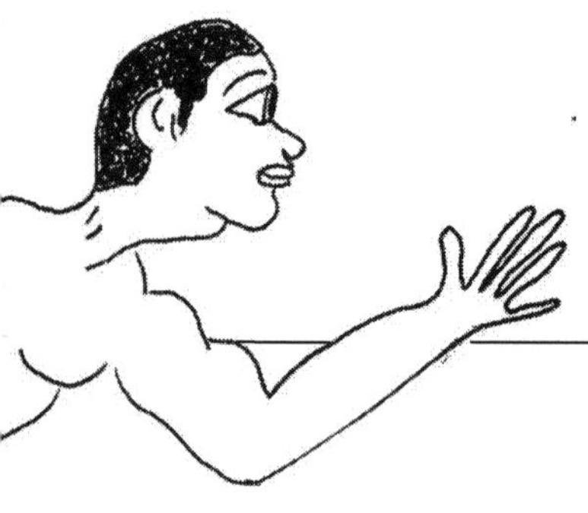

There may no longer be segregation,
but redlining, even today, still *manifests.*

There may no longer be firemen
spraying at blacks,
but blacks are drenched with attack
during *protests.*

There may not be minstrels
and blackface,
but some blacks on tv
are made to look a foolish *mess.*

There may no longer be the false
"separate but equal",
but underfunded schools surely proves
this still *occurs.*

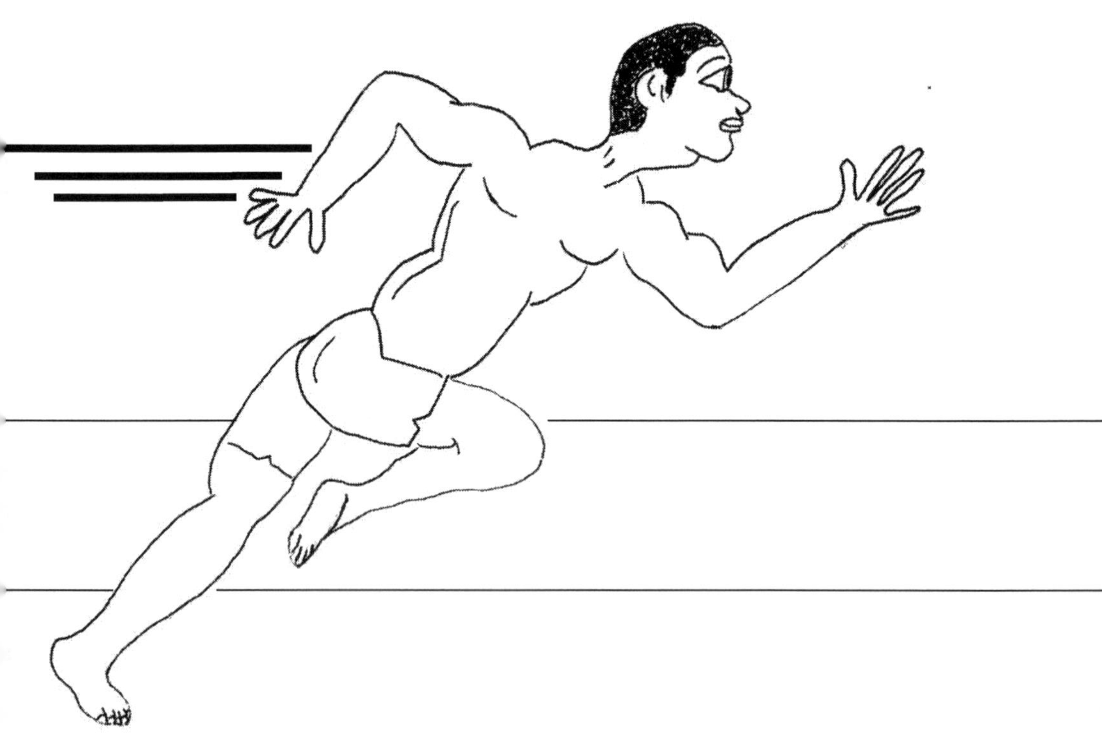

And there may no longer be
as many lynchings,
but police brutality
is the same with different *words.*

History is a WEAPON!

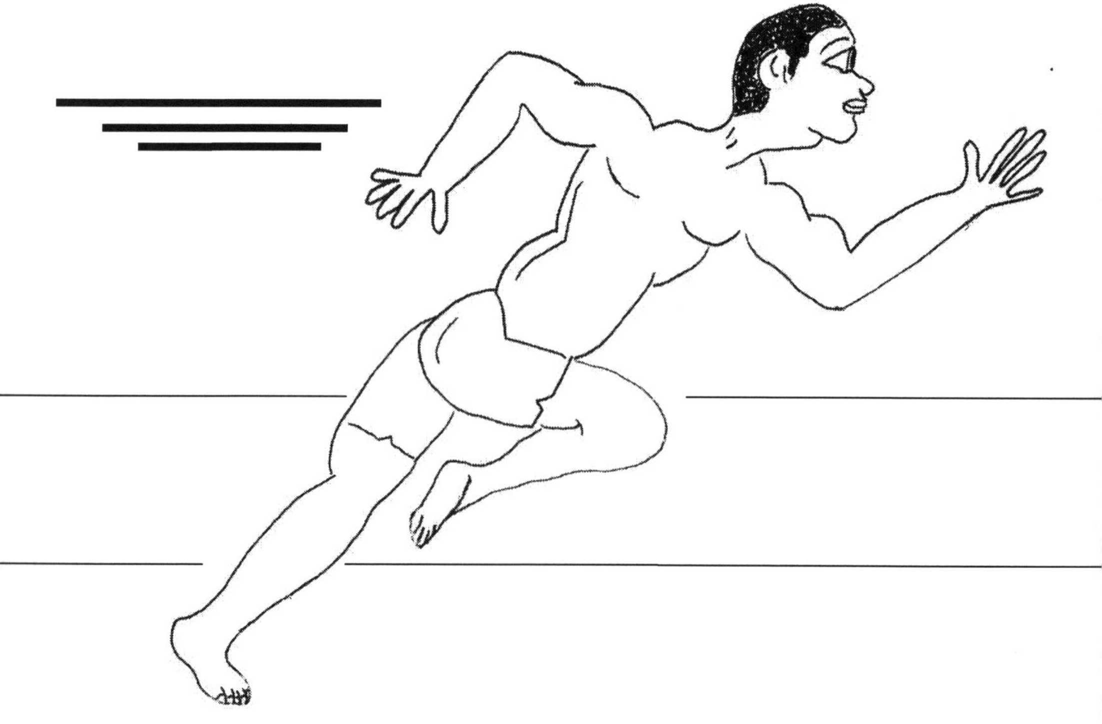

History is STRONG!

History is VITAL!

Learning history

DEFEATS

FUTURE

WRONGS!

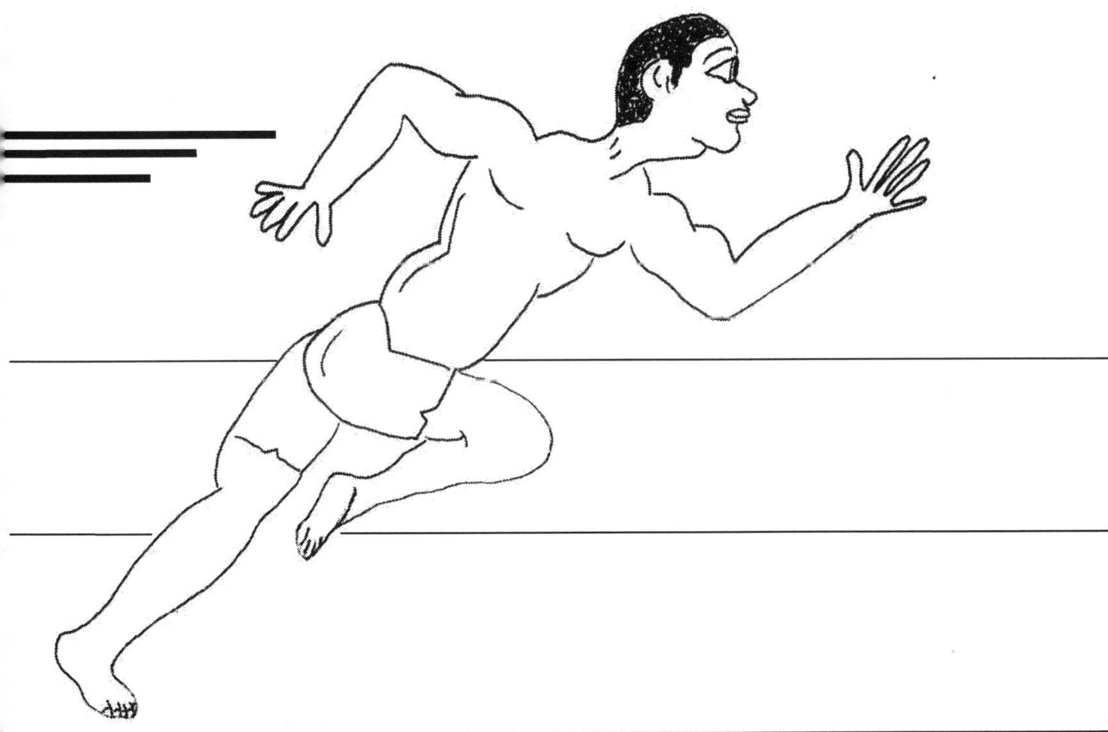

And although black people are not

exactly where they want to *be,*

still facing the stigma of their black skin,

they'll keep running to **overcome**

HISTORY!

Blacks stand on the shoulders

of their ancestors

and those that stand with pride and *glee,*

are compelled to reach

their greatest potential

as they run to **overcome**

HISTORY!

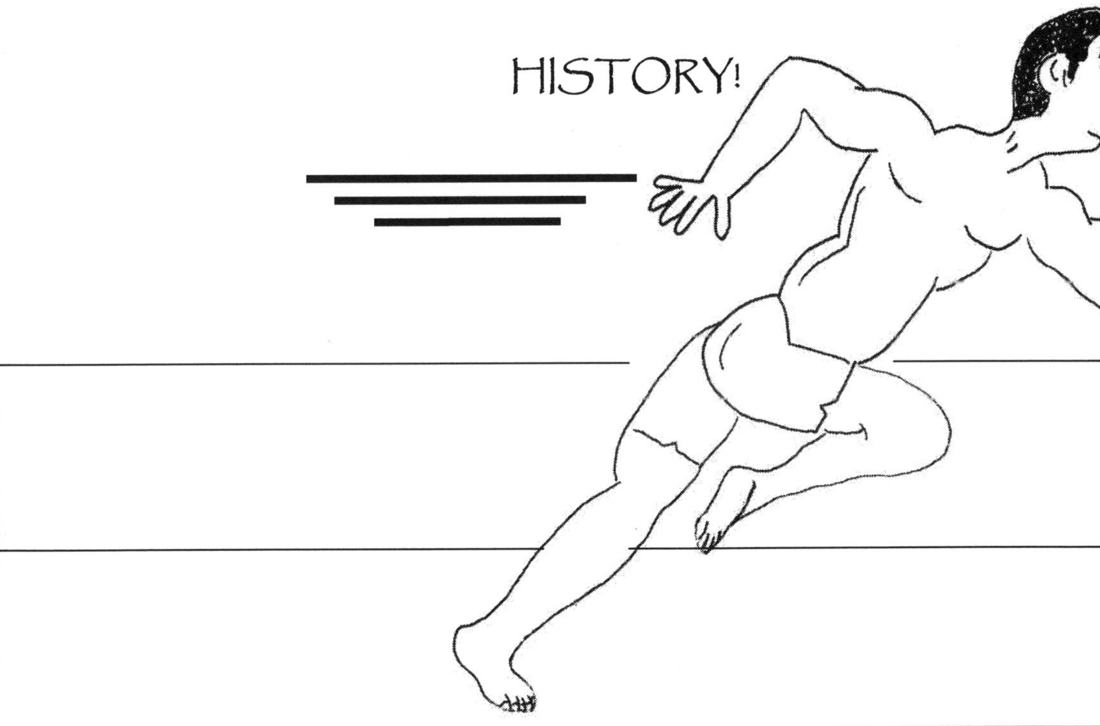

148

The End

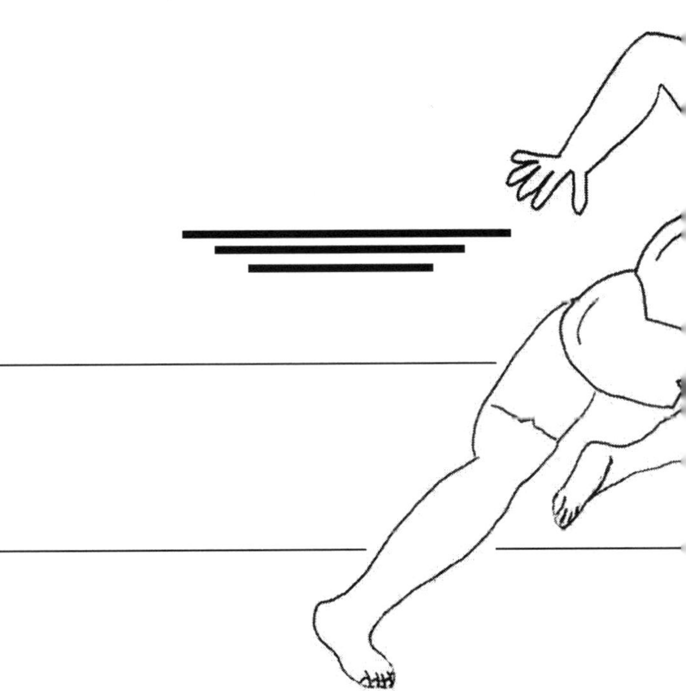

Not By Coincidence

They dunked my head in the water
and then asked me, "Why can't you breathe?"

They tripped me . I fell face first.
They asked me, "Why does your face bleed?"

They took my GPS
and asked me, "Why are you lost?"

They stepped on my head, neck and back
and asked, "Who's the boss?"

They took my shoes, jacket and clothes
and asked, "Why are you cold?"

I told them, "It all started the day...my history you stole."

Despite Because

Despite being enslaved,
blacks proved that they are strong.

Because they were enslaved
their strength shall overcome all the wrongs.

Despite being dehumanized,
blacks proved that they are strong.

Because they were dehumanized
their strength shall overcome all the wrongs.

Despite segregation,
blacks proved that they are strong.

Because of segregation
their strength shall overcome all the wrongs.

Despite unfair laws
blacks proved that they are strong.

Because of unfair laws
their strength shall overcome all the wrongs.

About the Author Nikki Ace

I am a mom.

I am not just any mom.

I am a black mom, married to a black man. I am also a parent of a black boy and a black girl.

Like so many others, I believed the false narrative of black history or lack thereof. And I refuse to have my children be misled.

You see, in school I was not told that Africans were a civilized and a cultured people in Africa before American slavery. I always believed the myth that black history began in America and that prior to their enslavement, Africans were **not** culturally advanced. So it wasn't worth mentioning. *I believed a lie.* I was also never told about the systemic unfair treatment of black people that still affect us to this present day. *I had been fooled.*

Now, just so you know, I have never been a lover of history. In fact, learning history felt like utter torture when I was younger. It was boring. It just honestly felt fictional to me. History was out of my reach and unrelatable. I couldn't exactly connect or comprehend how learning this information would help me today, let alone my future.

It also didn't help that most of my middle to high school curriculum did not include much *African-American* history - the history that looks like me. So I turned a blind eye to this subject. I only studied history to pass the test. Nothing more.

Fast forward to my college years and you will see that I definitely went through the common 'Red, Black and Green' phase as a student enrolled in Pan African Studies.

As I learned about the unrelenting injustice done to black people through class discussions, reading books, studying photographs, and viewing required videos for assignments, I initially got 'Red' with anger. The blinders I used to cover my interest in history were now lifted and so was my right fist in honor of black pride.

Then I went into the 'Black' phase where my anger subsided. But I was definitely 'woke'. I was clearly conscious of some, *not all*, racial discrimination in society.

And finally, I reached the 'Green' phase where I would hypothetically sing *'We are the World'* and if I am being truly honest, I was still a little alert to discrimination. However, I do believe that I became less attentive to the black experience as a whole.

Not until I became a mother did I fully realize how deliberate I need to be to ensure my children know the impact of their history:

'How it can bring a sense of pride...'

'How you can get a better understanding of why things are the way that they are nowadays...'

'Why people treat you the way they do...'

'Why everyone is not on a level playing field...'

'*How not to allow the atrocities in history repeat itself...*'

and '*What is needed to move forward* . . . etc.'

Although this history can be painful, it is beautiful at the same time. The triumphs within the tragedies demonstrates the strength, resilience and tenacity of black people.

While standing on the shoulders of our ancestors, my hope is that my children will say *"I can't"* less and say *"I can"* more.

I long for my children to fully grasp the fact that stereotypes will program the way some people may see them and not always in the best way.

I need to equip my children for a world that will **judge them unfairly** simply because of the color of their skin.

I need to prepare them for a world that might **fear them** simply because of the color of their skin.

And I need to raise them to be **confident** in the very skin they are in, by teaching them the courage and grit of their predecessors.

Some people try to teach their children how to live in a world of color blindness, however this is a misleading ideal. People need to realize that the differences in our color is a clear indication of the certain privileges and opportunities certain people have that others don't. It shouldn't be this way. But it is. **To pretend color doesn't exist, does not bring resolve.** There is nothing wrong with my color, so why would some choose to be "blind" to it? Why would some choose *to not* see the beauty of my color? To see color and respond in a way that is not discriminatory, but loving and accepting, is the way to go. And I want my children to see...The Beauty. In. Every. Color. Of. The. Rainbow.

So, I am learning history with my children. **I am by no means a scholar of history.** But what I am, is a mom that wants to set her children up for the highest opportunity for success. And to be honest, I am setting myself up to reach my own greatest potential.

My desire with this book is to enlighten. Inform. And empower others. So as I continue to learn... I will write. As I continue to discover new information, my family will keep on hearing my shocking gasps shrieking through the walls from the other room.

No matter what, I am proud to say that I am raising conscious children that will know the truth about their black heritage. **I even believe that this knowledge is key to developing healthy relationships with people of every race. Every ethnicity. Every color. And every nationality.**

I've realized that our history isn't just one or two people that wanted to discriminate against black people for whatever reason. This problem is *systemic* and *structural*. This history is essential for every child and adult to learn to be the change in our *system* that we want to see in the world. When children and adults can see the extraordinary in themselves, then they can see the extraordinary in others that look like them.

First and foremost, I want my children to fully celebrate the fact that they are each a 'descendant of royalty'. Royalty blood runs fervently through their veins. Not only do they have ancestors that are royalty, but they were created by the King of Kings and the Lord of Lords. This makes them regal. Majestic. And to put it simply, they are important. They will be confident in knowing that this royalty symbolizes strength. Vigor. And perseverance unparalleled. The survival and persistent stride of a people that keep getting knocked down . . . **this . . . this . . . this is true royalty!**

"It is easier to build strong children than to repair broken men."

-Frederick Douglas

Vocabulary

Head Start - *an early start* that gives an advantage or *a productive start* given in any endeavor

Corridors of power - the highest level of authority (which are typically occupied by white people)

Slavery – the practice of forcing involuntary labor on other people and dominating them under terrible conditions---- American slavery was implemented by a system of endless rough treatment, long and heavy work, rape, threats, torture and murder of black people for profit.

Chattel slavery – a method of slavery where human beings are considered *personal property* and sold as if they were a *product*

The System – a strong government or social organization that designed a set of rules and practices that work toward a collective goal

Systemic racism - refers to the policies and procedures that are set up to perpetuate racial inequity

Structural racism - refers to a system that can be social, economic or even political that are habitually practiced where white people have received *more opportunities* and black people have *less opportunities* on the basis of race

Racial equity - the allocation of society's benefits and inconveniences that are *not* influenced by race

Perseverance - despite challenges, to still persist

Caste – any group of people (i.e. racial group) that receive special rights and opportunities or a group (i.e. racial group) that are believed to be clearly different socially--- Groups that are considered to be a part of a *"higher caste"* experience more privileges than those that are on a *"lower caste"*.

Segregation – the act of separating a person, group (i.e. racial group) or thing with the purpose of keeping them apart, but unfortunately one group is treated unfairly

Marginalization – when a group of people are put down as inferior and therefore are excluded and/or treated as insignificant

Integration – the process when a group (i.e. racial group) is accepted into joining another community --- The purpose of integration is to bring equality.

Suffrage – the right to vote

Disenfranchisement - the act of *not allowing* a person or group of people (i.e. racial group) certain privileges and depriving them of the right to vote.

Hurdle #1

The Capture

Questions to Discuss

What was life like for Africans prior to being enslaved in the Americas?

When we think about Africa today, Africa is *only* shown to be a place where there are children and adults that are diseased, famine is rampant and there are wars... followed by wars... followed by more wars. We have also been given the idea that Africans are sort of like primitive brutes and savages that are uncivilized amongst wild animals. To say the least, Africans have been given a negative narrative for the longest time. Some people have even argued that black people should be happy that they were enslaved because Africa was and *still is* unsophisticated.

This could not be further from the truth. First of all, the origin of *all human life* **originated in Africa.** Africa is the second largest continent in the world, being very diverse with thousands of different ethnic groups and thousands of languages. There is proof of amazing advancements in the areas of science, math, technology, medicine and a myriad of artifacts that display beautiful artistic creations. Africans were skilled in architecture, engineering, construction work, ironmaking, ivory carving, pottery, rope and gum production, not to mention an abundance of other technological advances. The government structures were organized. There were sophisticated cities and towns. And various religions were practiced.

Africa has so many achievements that have been untold. Don't allow yourself to be deceived that Africa was a land of nothingness and nothing people.

(Source: The Abolition Movement
"Africa Before Transatlantic Slavery"
http://abolition.e2bn.org/slavery_41.html)

Was there slavery in Africa prior to American slavery?

Yes, there was. As you study history, you will see that slavery was often a system used in various places around the world.

How was the slavery in Africa different than the slavery in America?

Slavery in every sense of the word is always a bad condition to be in, however my research shows that slavery in Africa was largely *not* like the chattel slavery (slaves treated as personal property) that was so prevalent in America.

***African slaves in Africa were *taken prisoner in battle,* as a result of criminal behavior, *or when a debt owed,* etc...

***slavery had a time limit. It wasn't forever.
***sometimes freedom could be bought, which is similar to indentured servitude
***many slaves ate the same food as the enslavers
***children were not automatically enslaved when born from a parent that was enslaved
***slaves in Africa were **seen as humans** and given more rights than those who were enslaved in America
***in some cases, enslaved Africans would be considered part of the family, however they were not allowed to leave the compound

(Source: PORTCITIES: Bristol
"Slavery in Africa"
http://www.discoveringbristol.org.uk/slavery/people-involved/enslaved-people/enslaved-africans/africa-slavery/)

The Native Americans lived in close proximity to these settlers entering the New World. Were they also enslaved?

Yes. Native Americans were enslaved in the New World and also sent to other places. It is my understanding that the declining of Native American slavery and the rise of African chattel slavery was due to a couple of reasons. Many of the Native Americans, already living in the New World, were very familiar with the terrain of the land. This knowledge allowed them to flee away from these invaders effectively.

Also, many Native Americans died off because of **epidemic diseases** that Europeans brought. Since there was such a decrease of Native Americans, they needed Africans to do the hard labor.

(Source: "Indian Enslavement in Virginia"
https://www.encyclopediavirginia.org/indian_enslavement_in_virginia)

"...2.5 to 5 million Native Americans (were) enslaved throughout the Americas since Columbus to 1900."

- Andrés Reséndez, Phd
Historian at the University of California Davis
Author of The Other Slavery: The Uncovered Story of Indian Enslavement in America

Which European nations were responsible for enslaving Africans during the Trans-Atlantic Slave Trade?

The European nations involved in the enslavement of Africans were **Portugal**, **Spain**, **Britain**, **France**, the **Netherlands**, **Denmark** and **Sweden**.

(Source: Liver Pool Museums
"European Traders"
https://www.liverpoolmuseums.org.uk/ism/slavery/europe/index.aspx)

Why did Europeans want to enslave Africans in particular?

To meet the demand for domestic servitude and the intense labor of growing and harvesting profitable crops, Europeans looked to Africans as their prized labor force. It is my understanding that Europeans were keenly aware of the **skills** Africans had and how they were acclimated to working in harsh weather conditions. This made them the "perfect" choice to help this New World grow its wealth while using an unpaid labor force.

Africans were also taken from the *west part of Africa* because of the convenience for ships landing at sea ports. It provided accessibility for ships traveling from Europe to Africa —and then to the American colonies —and back to Europe.

Finally, it is also believed that Africans were chosen because it would be more difficult for them to escape because of their **unfamiliarity** of the land. If they were to escape, their distinct dark **skin** and features wouldn't allow them to blend in with anyone else. So, they couldn't hide.
(So-called "Christian" Europeans also missioned to save Africans with their twisted and warped belief of Christianity.)

(Source: PBS
"Why Did Europeans Enslave Africans?"
https://www.pbs.org/video/why-did-europeans-enslave-africans-srl1wr/)

Other than the United States of America, where else were Africans taken during the Trans-Atlantic Slave Trade?

Most Africans were shipped to the **Caribbean** (roughly more than 4,000,000). Africans were also shipped to **Brazil** (roughly 4,000,000) while the least amount of slaves were shipped to the **United States** (roughly 400,000).

(Source: Encyclopedia Virginia
"The Transatlantic Slave Trade"
https://www.encyclopediavirginia.org/Transatlantic_Slave_Trade_The)

What was the long time demographic impact on Africa?

Since many slave traders captured Africa's physically powerful men and women to be sold to Europeans, Africa was depleted of a strong defense to protect itself from danger. This left many parts of Africa vulnerable to being taken over and being colonized.

(Source: TED-Ed
"The Atlantic Slave Trade"
https://ed.ted.com/lessons/the-atlantic-slave-trade-what-your-textbook-never-told-you-anthony-hazard)

Which crops were the most profitable for white land owners?

The profitable crops in North America were **cotton**, **rice**, **tobacco** and even **indigo**.

What's indigo, you ask?

Well, indigo is a plant that produces a dye the color blue. This plant was rare, so it was expensive which meant only the elite could buy it. They used this dye to color textiles.

(Source: Ancestry.com
"Growing Indigo in South Carolina"
http://www.ancestry.com/historicalinsights/indigo-south-carolina)

Most Africans were shipped to the Caribbean and Brazil to be enslaved. The main cash crops in the Caribbean and Brazil were the **sugar cane**, **coffee**, **indigo** and **rice**. These cash crops grew well in the climate in Brazil and the Caribbean. These early settlers would create plantations and sell the crops to Europeans for a hefty financial profit. Also, working on the sugar cane plantations was so strenuous that many slaves didn't live that long. This created a greater demand for more slaves to be shipped.

(Source: Colonial Williamsburg
"Slavery and Remembrance"
http://slaveryandremembrance.org/articles/article/?id=A0011)

How did the Europeans capture Africans in Africa?

Africa has always been a land of diverse people. This continent has a myriad of different ethnic groups. People speak different languages. And there's an array of countless tribes.

During the time Europeans showed interest in enslaving Africans, these tribes would fight. Have wars. And they would hold their enemies captive. Groups of slave merchants would also target villagers from other tribes and capture them. These are the people African merchants would then sell to Europeans slave traders.

African merchants **were not selling** their mothers, fathers, sisters, brothers or allies as many are led to believe. (Also, please note that wars, rivalries and prisoners of war are not an uncommon practice for people on the same continent. So this was not odd behavior. Just thought you should know.)

Europeans were not fully capable of kidnapping as many Africans that they needed. Therefore, they highly depended on these African merchants. However, Europeans did do their share of African raiding.

The myth that *Africans sold their own people* seems to be a way to point blame away from Europeans. It's quite deflective. Just to be clear, there was no loyalty expected from rival tribes.

To make this point crystal clear, let's take a quick look back between 1932-1945 during World War II when the Japanese enslaved Chinese and Korean women as comfort women. No one says that they enslaved their own people. They are all on the same continent. Just as Africans. These are people that are seen as distinctly different from each other. Africans from different tribe should also be seen as distinctly different from each other. Because they are.

(Source: Digital History
"Enslavement"
http://www.digitalhistory.uh.edu/disp_textbook.cfm?smtid=2&psid=445)

What did the Europeans trade for the African captives?

Europeans traded **iron**, ***guns***, **gunpowder**, **mirrors**, **copper**, **knives**, **cloth**, **textiles**, **wine**, **trinkets**, **jewelry**, **beads** . . . among other goods for African captives.

(Source: Wikipedia
"Triangular Trade"
https://en.wikipedia.org/wiki/Triangular_trade)

How were Africans typically placed on ships?

Europeans would overload ships with hundreds of Africans. They were packed so close that it was similar to how you would **pack spoons**. They were chained together and could hardly turn left or right. Each cell was so low that they **couldn't sit up**. If they had to use the restroom, they had to go where they sat or laid. As you can imagine, this created an even more dreadful experience and many got sick and died. Africans that got sick were **thrown overboard** to prevent the spreading of their illness.

(Source: History Channel
"Life Aboard a Slave Ship"
https://www.youtube.com/watch?v=PmQvofAiZGA)

What was the Transatlantic Slave Trade?

The **Transatlantic Slave Trade** comprised of the transportation of goods brought by ship *from* Europe... *to* Africa ... to trade for African captives. These Europeans brought these Africans *to* the Americas... and then a ship would *return to* Europe with goods from the Americas to be sold in Europe. And repeat... and repeat... and repeat.

There were about **54,000 voyages** in the Transatlantic Slave Trade with over 12 million Africans being transported to mostly the Caribbean, Brazil and less Africans being sent to North America. (It is estimated that over 2 million of the 12 million died while being transported.)

(Source: "The Story of Africa" http://www.bbc.co.uk/worldservice/specials/1624_story_of_africa/page53.shtml)

Hurdle #2

Enslavement

Questions to Discuss

How did slavery benefit white people?

Money! **$** Money! **$** Money! **$** Mo----ney! **$**

Slavery was about economics. Slavery was a business. It provided a huge, profitable economic base for **southern** white plantation owners and **northerners** also benefitted financially off of the backs of slaves.

The flat land in the south was conducive for farming which is why white landowners built plantations. 'Cash crops' such as cotton, sugar, rice and tobacco were harvested on this land to be sold for profit.

Although slavery was not as prevalent in the north as in the south, it did exist and northerners definitely benefited financially from slave labor. In fact, the New England colonies, which are located in the north, were active in ship building for the transfer of Africans to the Americas and also to help trade other goods. Additionally, the cotton that slaves picked would be sent to the north to be made into textiles for profit.

(Source: "Europeans Come to Western Africa"
https://www.pbs.org/wgbh/aia/part1/1narr1.html)

"For the love of money is a root of all kinds of evil, for which some have strayed from the faith in their greediness, and pierced themselves through with many sorrows."

-1 Timothy 6:10

Slavery happened a long time ago. Why are you bringing this up?

Let me make this really clear to you. The institution of slavery still exists. But it goes by different names.

"Slavery did not end in 1865 . . .
it just simply evolved."

-Bryan Stevenson
Author of <u>Just Mercy</u>

"Slavery went from being physical to being mental."

-Dick Gregory
American Comedian and Civil Rights Activist

"Prior to one hundred years ago, they didn't need tricks. They had chains. And they needed the chains because you and I hadn't been brainwashed thoroughly enough to submit to their brutal acts of violence submissively. ... And it was only after the spirit of the black man was completely destroyed, then they had to use different tricks. They just took the **physical** *chains from his ankles and put them on his* **mind."**

-Malcolm X
Human Rights Activist

What does race have to do with slavery?

Slavery was a system that was predicated upon the idea that one group of people *-established by apparent physical features and differences-* are somehow **suitable for enslavement** in ways that other people are not. And this is how race became a huge contributing factor on how people would be treated and chosen to be enslaved.

Being black qualified someone for subordination to enslavement and being white, in contrast, kept one exempt from that subordination to enslavement.

How does a narrative impact a person's belief?

A **narrative** is defined as a spoken or written account of connected events. It is also defined as a story. Narratives that still impact attitudes today (that began with slavery) is that black people are *innately different. Less than human. Inferior. Not hard workers. And not as intelligent in comparison to others.*

White people that believed this narrative were able to somehow rationalize why blacks should be enslaved. This belief system still influences modern America today. Unfortunately, even some black people have bought into this negative narrative. We have created our own biases on our own people. Yikes! This is a dangerous place to be, which is why so many black people are working so hard to demonstrate counter-narratives by sharing positive truths.

For one, our past history is told as 'His Story'.

Not 'Black People's Story'.

From a black person's perspective.

'His Story' is a version of history that the *'corridors of power'* (the highest level of authority which is typically occupied by white people) want us to believe.

Black history has not been shared with an accurate narrative because of *who* had the most power to share and tell the stories (or choose not to share). We have been taught a history that *vilifies* the *victimized* and *makes heroes* out of *oppressors*.

This is contradictory to what is supposed to be American values and I want our past to be told to help others understand who they are. What really happened. And how "history" is still here. Even today.

"American has been sold a bill of goods through false advertising: the myth of black inferiority...
Media...is the messenger...
It carries out the myth of black inferiority."

-Tom Burrell
Author of Brainwashed

What impact did the narrative about Africa have on black people?

Malcolm X said there has been so many negative things said about Africa to such a degree, that blacks- themselves- didn't want to have anything to do with Africa. We end up **hating ourselves.**

"You can't hate the roots of a tree and not hate the tree. You can't hate your origin without hating yourself. You can't hate Africa and not hate yourself."

He then explains how black people have been brainwashed. The white man clearly knows that black people's positive attitude towards their history will create a positive attitude about themselves.

"They very skillfully make us hate our African identity...characteristics (like body features)... our black skin...it made us feel inferior, inadequate ..."

-Malcolm X
Human Rights Activist

Why did white people erase Africans past from history?

I believe that there is a complete psychology when it comes to slavery. White enslavers clearly knew how to break down the mindset of people. They knew that if they could control the mind, that everything else physically will be under their power. If a human being is taken from their homeland. Away from their loving family. And having their culture stripped away. It is only a short amount of time before they start to see themselves as nothing more than a commodity and not a human being.

"When people have a history...that makes you a
somebody.
So if you remove the history...you become a
nobody.
Your history (is) disappearing . . . nobody's lamenting the loss of that history. That's why . . . colonizers and enslavers make the people whose history they've conquered . . . disappear."

-Robin Walker
Historian
aka The Black History Man

What was unique about black enslavement in America?

"There is only one group of people who had the peculiar experience of being **unfree** *in a* **free** *land... and that's African Americans."*

-Ken Burns,
Documentarian, American Filmmaker

What was slave life like?

From the time the *sun rose* in the morning to the time the *sun set* in the evening was the work day schedule for many slaves working in the fields. To ensure "productivity", they were under **constant surveillance** of overseers. And if their work ethics appeared to be slacking, they were punished. Even if their work ethic was meticulous, they could be "punished" just to induce fear in the mind of the enslaved.

House slaves had domestic chores and were always expected to work in clear view sight of slave owners. Children that were enslaved were also expected to work in the fields alongside the adults. Furthermore, black children were often called the **property of white** children even if the white child was younger. Some black children were even purchased to simply be a playmate for white children; however blacks were not afforded the same rights such as attending school.

Plus, black men and women could not legally get married. But they didn't let this stop them. They created their own ceremony where they would jump over a broom together symbolizing their new union. This is a popular tradition that black couples today still do at their wedding to pay honor to ancestors.

(Source: Ebony
"Jumping the Broom"
https://www.ebony.com/life/white-people-jumping-the-broom-marriage/)

It was also **illegal** for the enslaved to receive an education to learn **to read or write**. A slave would be punished for attempting to read a book. Even white people that were caught teaching the enslaved how to read or write could be reprimanded. Those enslaved that did know how to read or write were sometimes secretly taught by a sympathetic white person they came in contact with. This black individual would educate other blacks while continuing to teach themselves with the basic skills they had.

Among the many prohibitions was banning slaves from being able to vote and owning property. On the whole, black people were prevented from being their best selves and their inability to contribute freely ends up hurting everyone. They had so much more they could have offered. But couldn't.

(Source: Library of Congress
"Pre-Civil War African-American Slavery"
http://www.loc.gov/teachers/classroommaterials/presentationsandactivitie
s/presentations/timeline/expref/slavery/)

Why was it illegal for slaves to receive an education?

"When you learn this history, you have an empowerment. ... We're the the only race of people in the history of the United States for whom it was illegal to read or write... There was an understanding that ***EDUCATION*** *led to a* ***RESISTANCE****. You would not accept your condition if you knew how your condition was created."*

- Nikole Hannah – Jones

Journalist behind New York Times Magazine's 1619 Project

Who was Harriet Tubman?

Harriet Tubman (also known as Moses) was a conductor of the Underground Railroad. She is legendary for her bravery and courage when she escaped from slavery to free land in 1849 to Philadelphia, Pennsylvania.

She selflessly went back to the south on multiple trips to sneakily help about 300 other slaves escape. One way, among many other ways, of helping slaves escape, was by being cunning. Harriet Tubman was just that.

Not only would Harriet Tubman disguise herself as a man, but she would additionally walk past plantations singing ***African-American spirituals*** (also known as Negro Spirituals) such as "Steal Away to Jesus" or "Go down, Moses". These songs were secret language to rally slaves that were interested in escaping to the north.

(Source: Library of Congress
"African-American Spirituals"
https://www.loc.gov/item/ihas.200197495/)

When slaves would successfully escape to the North, could they be enslaved again?

The **Fugitive Slave Law of 1850** allowed slavecatchers in the south to capture escaped slaves in the north and bring them back to enslavement. Those in the north would also be expected to return escaped slaves to their so-called rightful "owners", since these human beings were seen as personal property.

(Source: "Fugitive Slave Act of 1850"
https://en.wikipedia.org/wiki/Fugitive_Slave_Act_of_1850)

What did slaveholders do to keep enslaved blacks under "control"?

The **"Willie Lynch" letter** is documentation of a speech addressing slave owners that needed advice on how to control slaves. Its purpose is to explain the psychology of how to keep enslaved black people under control by 'breaking them down'. Some deem that this letter is a **hoax** and that the speaker, supposedly a slave owner named "Willie Lynch", actually never existed.

Now, although this "Willie Lynch" Letter has not been proven to be true, I do think it is worth examining since many of the tactics explained were actually carried out during slavery.

According to "Willie Lynch", in order to control the enslaved people, you must dismantle them mentally.

This was achieved:
* with constant abuse in clear view eye sight of the other enslaved individuals
* by creating discord amongst blacks so that they fight with each other
* separating families
* by imparting fear in the enslaved so that they will be discouraged from being rebellious

(Source: The Willie Lynch Letter and the Making of a Slave written by "Willie Lynch")

If a slave was caught running away, what might be the consequence?

If slaves were caught running away, some slaveholders would have them wear a **metal slave collar** around their neck that had bells on it. If they ever tried to escape again, overseers could hear them running away. So, the bells were extremely functional. There were also other metal slave collars that had long hooks to prevent slaves from being able to run away in the woods.

How were blacks treated in the northern states as compared to the southern states?

Slavery was heavily a southern matter more than the north, but bigotry was truly an issue for the entire nation in all of America. I remember being told that the south didn't care that blacks were close...just as long as they didn't get too big. The north didn't care how big blacks got...as long as they didn't get too close. So, whether you are black in the north or black in the south, you were treated unfairly.

"If you're black, you were born in jail, in the north as well as the south. Stop talking about the south. Long as you south of the Canadian border, you're south."

-Malcolm X
Human Rights Activist

What are some of the ways blacks were dehumanized?

White people had to see blacks as something that was not human in order to justify enslaving them. They needed a way to ease their own consciousness. One way that this mentality of believing black people weren't human is when blacks would be used for experimentation. Yes, experimentation. Just as you would for a lab rat.

#1*****Dr. James Marion Sims** has been honored in the field of surgery; however he would perform surgery on slave women without anesthesia to find the cure for a complication affecting women. He didn't use anesthesia because he believed blacks had a super endurance to pain. To say the least, his surgical practices were extremely painful. ▪ And yes, these black women suffered a lot of PAIN. Why? *Because they are human! And humans feel PAIN!*

#2***There was also an enslaved man named **John Brown** that recounted his enslavement in a book where he underwent agonizing tests. These tests were performed by a physician to prove that black skin is thicker than white skin. This physician would conduct a series of tests that would burn beneath his skin. Again, there is the belief that black people have a super high endurance for pain. And yes, he was in a lot of PAIN. Why? *Because he is human! And humans feel PAIN!*

Especially when they are being burned!

(Source: "1619 Project"- Linda Villarosa, Professor, The City College of New York- https://www.youtube.com/watch?v=8DqdPyHnb_o)

#3***These experimentations continued on even post slavery. The **Tuskegee Experiment** occurred between 1932-1972. Some poor black men (typically sharecroppers) had a disease called syphilis. These black men *were not treated* for this disease on purpose so that the researchers could study the progression of the disease. Some ended up having serious health conditions, spread the disease to their family and others died. This was yet another dehumanizing and <u>PAINFUL</u> practice.

#4***In addition to dehumanizing black people through experimentation, in 1787 there was a negotiation implemented called the **Three-Fifths Compromise**.

States in the south wanted to be represented more in Congress, but they needed to have a big population of people to be counted.

This would allow the south to secure more individuals with similar interests to be seated in Congress. The North did not want the slaves to be counted because they feared the southern states would eventually overpower the north, so they met in the middle and came up with this agreement.

This clause literally states that representation in Congress and taxation will be determined by "the whole number of free persons" and "three-fifth of all other persons" (the enslaved). This means that for every 5 slaves, only 3 slaves can be counted as people. Wow! A *whole person* has been reduced down to a *fraction of a person*. Imagine that.

(Source: "United States Constitution"
https://www.census.gov/history/pdf/Article_1_Section_2.pdf)

Was Nat Turner the only one to rebel against the brutality of slavery ?

Nope. Certainly not. There were many rebellions that came in various forms (poisoning slave owners food, setting the field on fire, etc...), however I'll just mention a couple more.

..

Denmark Vessey was responsible for spearheading the planning of a slave rebellion in South Carolina in 1822. He was a tenacious leader arranging an uprising that included 9,000 like-minded individuals desiring to abolish slavery. Sadly, a couple of slaves that were loyal to their slave masters *snitched* by exposing the plan to revolt. Needless to say, Denmark Vessey's plan could not be carried out.

Furthermore, one of the most (if not the only) successful slave rebellion was the **Haitian Revolution** which took place in a Caribbean Country called Haiti. In 1791, Africans in Haiti revolted against French colonial rule. And these Africans in Haiti won!

Did all <u>white abolitionists</u> (white people that wanted to get rid of slavery) believe in equal rights for black people?

No! In fact, the Great Emancipator, Abraham Lincoln, made it known that he was not a supporter for equal rights for blacks. He wanted to abolish slavery, but he didn't believe black people should have the same liberties and rights that whites have (for example, voting). He also said that he wanted to **send blacks away** to Africa (Liberia) or Central America because he believed blacks and white wouldn't be able to live pleasantly amongst each other.
Whoa! Surprise, surprise!

(Source: History.com
"5 Things You May Not Know About Abraham Lincoln, Slavery and Emancipation"
https://www.history.com/news/5-things-you-may-not-know-about-lincoln-slavery-and-emancipation)

Were there any <u>white people</u> that truly wanted to abolish slavery because of its immorality and believed in equal rights *for all*?

Yes! Of course there were. **John Brown** is the first to come to mind. He was a white man that abhorred slavery and the maltreatment of black people. He was a man willing to die for his strong belief in getting black people justice. And that's just what he did. He was compelled because he believed he was doing God's will. He is considered an extremely radical abolitionist because of the violent strategies that he used to help free the enslaved. He is well known for his 1859raid on Harper's Ferry in Virginia, which proved to be unsuccessful, but sent a strong message.
(This John Brown is *not to be confused* with the previously mentioned John Brown that was a black enslaved man experimented on.)

(Source: American Battlefield Trust
"John Brown"
https://www.battlefields.org/learn/biographies/john-brown)

Did any slaves ever try to sue in court to fight for their freedom?

#1***Elizabeth Freeman, better known as **Mum Bett** was a slave in the 1700s that disputed the presence of slavery in the state of Massachusetts. She expressed that slavery defies the values of the American Revolution.

Upon learning that the Massachusetts Constitution of 1780 stated that ***all human beings*** *were created equal and should be free*, she recognized the absurdity in her status and the status of white people. This Constitution stated ALL. She believed that ALL included herself and others enslaved.

She saw the irony in her enslavement and the basic American principles, so she sued in a county court with the help of a white lawyer named Theodore Sedgewick and won her freedom.

Mum Bett is known today as the **first** enslaved black person to file and **win a court case** on obtaining one's freedom in Massachusetts.

This groundbreaking case in 1781 is believed to be instrumental in abolishing slavery in Massachusetts.

(Source: National Women's History Museum
"Elizabeth Freeman"
https://www.womenshistory.org/education-resources/biographies/elizabeth-freeman)

#2***Isabella Baumfree, best known as **Sojourner Truth** was the first black woman to file a lawsuit against a white man and actually win the case.

Sojourner Truth was a former slave that had escaped with her infant, leaving behind her other children. Then her formal slave master illegally sold her 5 year old son, so she filed a lawsuit against him and won!

(Source: Biography
"Sojourner Truth"
https://www.biography.com/activist/sojourner-truth)

#3***One of the most infamous lawsuits was the **Dred Scott Case.** Dred Scott and his wife Harriet Scott were slaves that filed separate lawsuits to fight for their freedom. Dred Scott made a case that because he lived on land where slavery was illegal, he could never be enslaved again.

In 1857, the United States Supreme Court, in the ruling of *Dred Scott v. Sandford* declared that all blacks, no matter if they were free or enslaved, did not have the rights to citizenship and consequently could not sue in federal court. This was a long, tedious battle, since they first filed their lawsuits in 1846 (1846-1857). Unfortunately, the decision went against their hopes. **They did not win.** However, three months after this decision was made, their slave owner gave Dred Scott and his family the freedom they longed for.

(Source: History.com
"Dred Scott Case"
https://www.history.com/topics/black-history/dred-scott-case)

What is Juneteenth and why do people celebrate it?

Juneteenth is known as Freedom Day.

Initially, Abraham Lincoln issued the Emancipation Proclamation to *legally free* the slaves that lived in rebel Confederate states in 1863.

Congress passed the 13th Amendment on January 31, 1865 which abolished slavery all throughout the United States (except as punishment for a crime), however slave owners in Texas continued slave labor.

On top of this, the slaves were never told they were free.

So, on **June 19, 1865**, after the Civil War ended, General Granger (a federal troop from the north) publicized that slavery had been abolished.

Juneteenth is a day celebrated to commemorate the end of slavery!

(Note: Juneteenth = June + Nine*teenth*)

(Source: PBS - "What is Juneteenth?" https://www.pbs.org/wnet/african-americans-many-rivers-to-cross/history/what-is-juneteenth/)

When enslaved black people were emancipated, how did it impact the white former slave owners?

Blacks depended on whites, but many will argue that whites needed and depended on blacks even more. Basic tasks that slaves would do domestically or the hard labor was now the responsibility of white people to do independently. Whites had to learn how to do the slave labor they never had to do. This is why some whites would hire formerly enslaved blacks to do work at a very, very low pay.

Also, since black people could no longer be ***legally*** enslaved, many white people from the *'corridors of power'* down to a regular white citizen found no purpose for black existence. They felt blacks served no purpose after slavery and often made comments that blacks should just go back to Africa.

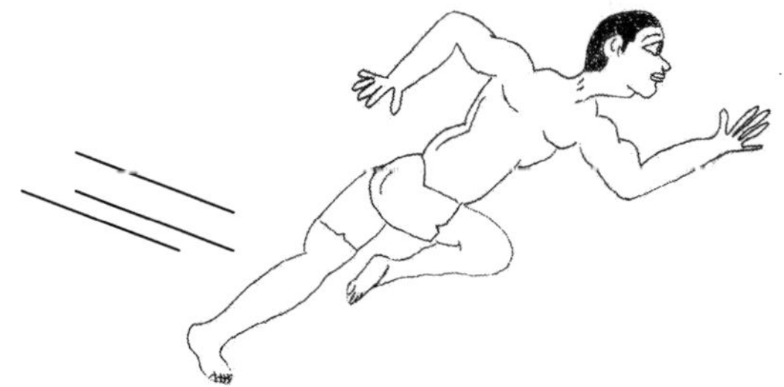

Hurdle #3

Reconstruction Era

Questions to Discuss

How did emancipation impact black people?

The **Reconstruction Era** began in 1865 and was set in motion after the American Civil War. This period was meant to be a time for America to rebuild. *Four million* enslaved blacks were now free and had to learn how to manage in their new liberated status. Upon being emancipated, many black people immediately searched for lost family members throughout the south. Many were without money. And we have to remember that enslaved persons were not allowed to read or write, so many were formally uneducated.

The **Freedmen's Bureau** was a saving grace for newly liberated black people, however it was a hit and a miss. It was established by Congress to help newly emancipated blacks and poor whites in the South in the after-effects of the American Civil War.

Knowing the transition from being enslaved to newly free would not be an easy task, this intervention administered aid such as housing, food and supplies. The agents sent from the north helped to negotiate contracts between employers and workers so that all is fair and square (as possible). Additionally, its support provided a more "peaceable" experience between southern whites and blacks.

Freedmen's Bureau also built hospitals, many schools and institutions of higher learning. In fact, a well-known **HBCU**

(Historically Black Colleges and Universities) named Howard University was named after a white Union general named Oliver Howard. He spearheaded the Freedmen's Bureau and was one of the founders of this university.

The Freedmen's Bureau was instrumental in helping black people organize and gain strength politically. Black men were given the right to vote in 1870 and boy, did they vote! Black men were voted as senators and even voted in Congress. However, this new wave of blackness on the political front gave rise to a white terrorist group called the **Ku Klux Klan**. Members of the Ku Klux Klan were white supremacists that would physically assault black people that were active politically and even whites that associated with these black people. As a response, the black vote decreased and so did future black politicians.

Unfortunately, the Freedmen's Bureau was not completely successful . It did not have all the support it needed. There was not enough funding to provide all the necessary provisions and the abandoned land that was planned to be given to the formerly enslaved, was given back to the white people that previously owned this land. This was an order made by President Andrew Johnson. So, black people were still without land ownership.

In an attempt to be able to work for money, since they could not own land, blacks would rent land from white land owners as **sharecroppers.** Black farmers would rent part of the land and rent supplies from owners as a loan. In many cases, this only added more frustration to black sharecroppers as many would find that the amount they harvested was not enough to pay the hefty loan they owe. They often profited little or nothing or were negative. This kept them **in debt** to white people, which is exactly the intent and strategy used to keep black people from moving ahead.

Regrettably, the Freedmen's Bureau ended in 1872, which was surely not enough time to recover from hundreds of years of enslavement.

(Source: History.com
"The Freedmen's Bureau"
https://www.history.com/topics/black-history/freedmens-bureau#section_3)

Why did black men start going to jail during the Reconstruction Era?

The 13th Amendment was signed in 1865 and officially approved after the American Civil War. It stated that:

"Neither slavery nor involuntary servitude, ***except as a punishment for crime*** *whereof the party shall have been duly convicted, shall exist within the United States."*

The loophole in this document allowed for the re-enslavement of black people in the form of **convict leasing**. Black people (mostly males, but also females) would be arrested and received a harsh punishment for minor crimes or even if they committed *no crime* at all.

Vagrancy laws were being strictly enforced. Blacks were criminalized if they were unable to prove that they had a job or if they simply... didn't have a job. They might also be *falsely accused* of owing a debt. A so-called white "debtor" would force a black person to work their debt off until the debt was fully paid. This is called *peonage.*

Convict leasing is where prisons would rent out prisoners as "slaves" to cover the cost for guarding and housing them *in exchange for* labor to private industries, coal mining companies, land owners and other corporations.

They would literally work them to death and when a worker died, it wasn't that big of a deal to these companies. Before, slaveholders made huge investments when they purchased slaves to "own". Unlike this previous chattel slavery, these imprisoned blacks were rented.

So when one dies.

They'll just go rent another one.

Yes, you read that correctly.

Rent!

As in rent a human being.

It's similar to how people treat rental cars. They will drive a rental car way worse than they would their own car because they have nothing invested in it. It's not their car, so they don't feel the need to take care of it by going slowly over bumps or avoiding potholes in the road. To them, the damage caused is someone else's problem, so in a way, convict leasing is seen as worse than slavery.

Local whites controlled the court system, so blacks were convicted often and in masses. This **criminalized** the black race and this only added to the narrative that blacks were *unlawful* and it was a *mistake to have freed the enslaved.*

(Source: Democracy Now!
"Michelle Alexander: Roots of Today's Mass Incarceration Crisis Date to Slavery, Jim Crow"
https://www.democracynow.org/2015/3/4/michelle_alexander_roots_of_todays_crisis)

What did the Black Codes do?

Black codes were passed without hesitation after the American Civil War beginning in 1865. It was intended to limit black people their rights and liberty while also having them work for low pay. It restricted black people the right to own property and to travel freely in the public domain.

(Source: Britannica "Black Codes"
https://www.britannica.com/topic/black-code)

Who is Jim Crow? What are Jim Crow laws?

Jim Crow was actually a character that a white actor in **black face** performed.

His name is Thomas Dartmouth Rice.

His **minstrel** routines were extremely racist as he would paint his face black and wear "slave-like" attire. He attempted to depict slaves as *ignoramus* by supposedly imitating their lifestyle and the way they would speak by sounding idiotic.

White people who have never been in contact with a black person were easily convinced that this was the way black people were in reality..

They believed the narrative that expressed black people as inferior and second rate.

And those that were fed this bait.

Snatched on quickly.

And passed on the message that black people were substandard.

This was all done by design.

WE SERVE WHITES ONLY

Jim Crow eventually became *synonymous* to **segregation**.

Jim Crow laws literally helped to deny basic human rights to black people.

Hospitals, restaurants, schools, churches, restrooms and even prisons were segregated – Blacks did not have the same access to facilities or other conveniences as whites, if they had any at all.

(Source: Khan Academy –
"The Origins of Jim Crow"
https://www.khanacademy.org/humanities/us-history/the-gilded-age/south-after-civil-war/v/jim-crow-part-1)

The laws of Jim Crow prevented white and black people from attending the same school. They were not even allowed to play games on the same playground, go to church, or take public transportation **together.** *Black people couldn't even swim in the same pool as white people. Water fountains were separated by race. Bathrooms were* **separated** *by race. And interracial relationships were strictly prohibited.*

– *Paraphrased from* –
Hoose, P. (2010).
<u>Claudette Colvin: Twice Toward Justice.</u>
Square Fish: New York, NY

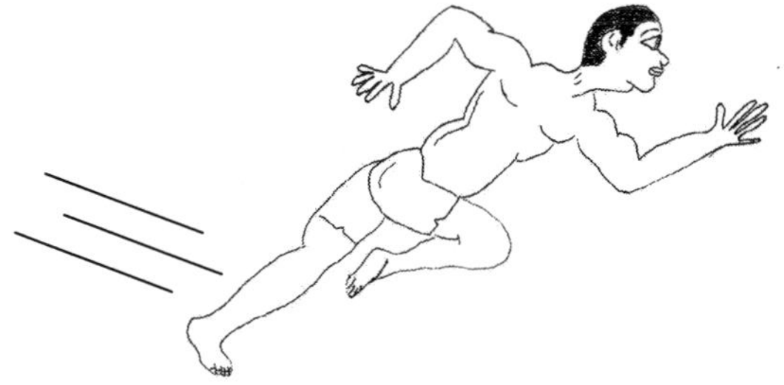

Hurdle #4

Bigotry

(racism, prejudice, intolerance)

Questions to Discuss

How was the government involved in Tulsa, Oklahoma's *Massacre of "Black Wall Street"* in the Greenwood District?

"People, some of them **agents of the government***, also deliberately burned or otherwise destroyed homes...churches, schools businesses, even a hospital and a library... in the Greenwood district. Despite duties to preserve order and to protect property, no government at any level offered adequate resistance, if any at all... people...numbering between 100-300, were killed during the massacre."*

As you can see, "agents of the government" <u>helped</u> in the destruction of this affluent black community.

(Source: "Tulsa Historical Society and Museum" https://www.tulsahistory.org/exhibit/1921-tulsa-race-massacre/)

Who received <u>reparations</u> after slavery ended?

Reparation is the action of repairing a wrong. White slaveholders received **reparations.** For each slave that they owned and freed, they received up to $300 for their "loss of property".

(Source: NY Times
"When Slave Owners Got Reparations"
https://www.nytimes.com/2019/04/16/opinion/when-slaveowners-got-reparations.html)

How did the Social Security Act of 1935 marginalize black people?

In 1935, the **Social Security Act** established "a system of *old-age benefits* for workers, benefits for victims of industrial accidents, unemployment insurance, aid for dependent mothers and children, the blind and the physically handicapped."

(Source: OurDocuments..gov
https://www.ourdocuments.gov/doc.php?flash=false&doc=68)

The Social Security Act of 1935 was signed into law by President Franklin D. Roosevelt, but he **omitted** agricultural and domestic workers that just so happened to be occupied by mostly black people. This exclusion led many people into thinking that this wasn't just by chance, but quite calculated.

This law really helped those that needed to retire- to still receive benefits so that they could continue their lifestyle. Unfortunately, far too many blacks were unable to benefit from this law and it has received criticism for **marginalization** (when a group of people are excluded and/or treated as insignificant).

(Source: Social Security Administration
https://www.ssa.gov/policy/docs/ssb/v70n4/v70n4p49.html)

Who created the Greenbook?

The Negro Motorist Greenbook was first published in 1936 by a man named Victor Green. He was a black mailman in New York. The Greenbook was a traveler's guide to help direct black people to locations that were welcoming to black people and not confrontational for black people.

(Source: History.com
https://www.history.com/news/the-green-book-the-black-travelers-guide-to-jim-crow-america)

How did the '*corridors of power*' show unfair practices when it came to housing?

A bias in the housing market was practiced through a process called **redlining**. Redlining was the practice where a red line was *literally* drawn on a map around areas that had a huge population of black people.

These areas would not be invested in and these black people were denied loans for mortgages on the basis of their race. Bank lenders also claimed that it would be too "risky" and "hazardous" to offer loans to black people.

Fortunately, the Fair Housing Act of 1968 prohibited lenders to use race as a determining factor for approving or denying an individual for a mortgage. *Unfortunately*, black people are still impacted by redlining today.

What is one of the main reasons there is so much of a wealth gap between the races in the USA?

Again. . .

One of the main reasons is because of **redlining.**

Homes in the suburbs were made unavailable for blacks to purchase (even if they could afford it) since the federal government prohibited blacks from home ownership in certain neighborhoods that were predominantly white.

On top of this, bank institutions would often deny black families a home loan to purchase a home.

White families that were able to buy homes in good neighborhoods gained over the next generations a vast amount of wealth because of home appreciation.

Black people were limited to renting homes and other public housing, so they were not able to gain **home equity** as whites have. Additionally, these black communities were inadequately invested in, which implied that unless you were wealthy , white or had power, you didn't matter much.

The Federal Government developed these entirely white suburbs and this is one of the many reasons there is such a huge wealth gap between whites and blacks.

"We have never remedied it and simply prohibiting future discrimination won't undo the effects of these policies."

-Richard Rothstein,
Author of The Color of Law: A Forgotten History of How Our Government Segregated America

One of the only ways to attempt to bridge this wealth gap is through **economic empowerment.** This is the ability to own and control valuable resources (land, business, etc.). For one, it's more difficult to progress as a renter. You are always under someone else's dominion when you don't own. And you will see some black people that appear to be closing this wealth gap, but it's kind of like increasing minimum wage. When pay increases, consumables and home prices also inflate, yet the rich keep getting richer and the gap keeps widening.

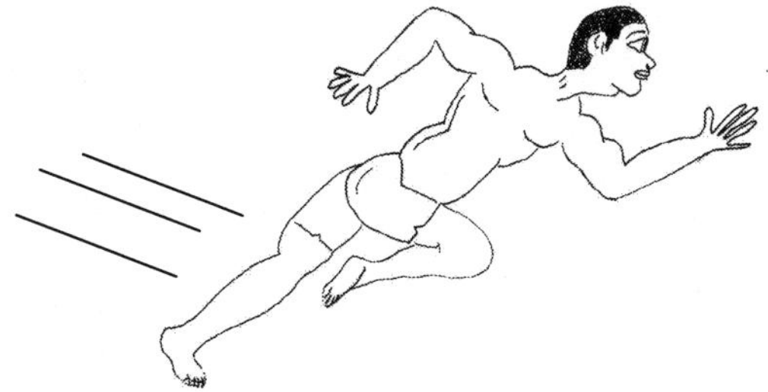

Hurdle #5

Integration

Questions to Discuss

If black people weren't being treated kindly by white people, why would they want to integrate schools?

Many black people wanted to integrate schools because all-white schools were better funded, had more qualified teachers, better resources, was less crowded, had nicer facilities and had better learning materials. Integrated learning was believed to offer more opportunities for black students.

The **1954 Brown vs. Board of Education** aimed to do all of these things to benefit black children. This was a case where 13 black students tried to enroll into all white schools and were denied admittance. After these parents took the Topeka Board of Education to court, the US Supreme Court found it to be unconstitutional to racially segregate schools.

(Source: "United States Courts"
https://www.uscourts.gov/educational-resources/educational-activities/history-brown-v-board-education-re-enactment)

What was the experience like for the first black students to attend an all-white school?

#1***The protests were so intense for the **Little Rock Nine** trying to attend Little Rock High School in Arkansas (1957) that President Eisenhower had to send Federal Troops to escort the nine black high school students to school for protection.

#2*****Dorothy Counts** was another student that was the first black person to attend an all-white school in Charlotte, North Carolina. White students responded to her presence by spitting on her and ridiculing her. Her teachers also didn't give her any attention. As you can imagine, her parents took her out of the school.

(Source: "Classmates screamed and spat at her. Sixty years later, she talks of forgiveness." https://www.charlotteobserver.com/news/local/article170707557.html)

What type of things would occur during a Sit-in Movement?

Sit-in demonstrations in the 1960s were performed by young black and even some white people (primarily black college students) at segregated lunch counters. These establishments refused to serve black people, so these demonstrators would simply sit at a lunch counter awaiting service.

Sit-ins were protests fighting for human rights and for everyone – *no matter their color*– to be seen as **equal citizens.**

They were devoted to the philosophy of non-violence, so when they would be thrown from their seats… or knocked to the ground… or had salt… pepper…milk… or hot coffee poured on their heads, they did not respond with hostility. And although they were not the aggressors, the sit-in demonstrators would be the ones arrested.

The effort of these demonstrations helped to bring national attention to the injustices happening in the south via the media. And their endeavors helped dismantle many legally sanctioned laws.

(Source: Stanford University
"Sit-ins"
https://kinginstitute.stanford.edu/encyclopedia/sit-ins)

How did the Freedom Riders contribute to the Civil Rights Movement?

In 1961, in an effort to put an end to segregation in the south, activists of multiple racial backgrounds... ages... gender... and religions rode on interstate buses together. The United States Supreme Court previously ruled that segregation in interstate commerce was unconstitutional. Despite this, southern segregationist did not abide by this rule. They abided by the Jim Crow laws that enforced segregation.

So, once the **Freedom Riders** hit the deep south, they were met with violent white mobs throwing rocks at their buses that broke windows, vicious attacks and imprisonment. And pardon me as I remind you...these riders were nonviolent.

Buses were even firebombed and destroyed. Again, I say...they were nonviolent.

Subsequently, their efforts gained a lot of media attention. This protest was successful in making its point of eliminating racial segregation. Later that year, the Interstate Commerce Commission made changes towards integration.

(Source: History.com
"Freedom Riders"
https://www.history.com/topics/black-history/freedom-rides)

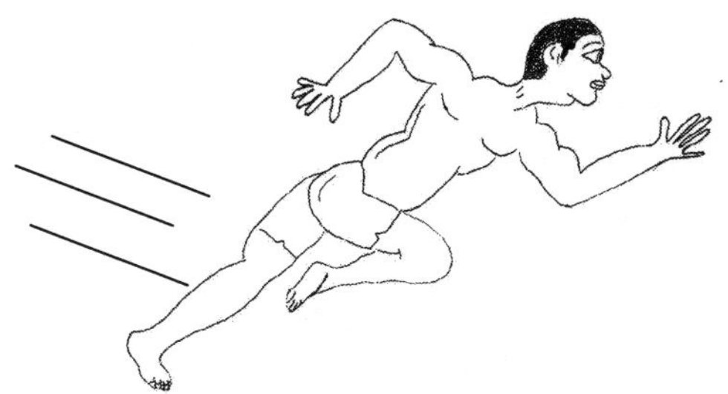

Hurdle #6

Activists' Plight

Questions to Discuss

Of course Rosa Parks was not the only black person that refused to give up her seat on the public bus. Who are some unsung heroes?

#1***Rosa Parks was not the first black person to refuse to give up her seat to a white person on the bus. Prior to Rosa Parks arrest on December 1, 1955, a 15- year old black girl named **Claudette Colvin** denied her seat on the bus and was arrested on March 2, 1955 in Montgomery, Alabama.

(Source: Wikipedia
"Claudette Colvin"
https://en.wikipedia.org/wiki/Claudette_Colvin)

#2***The infamous baseball player, **Jackie Robinson**, was also a forerunner for refusing to get up from his seat and go to the back of the military bus. In the month of July in 1944, he was arrested and court martialed.

(Source: THIRTEEN Media with Impact
https://www.thirteen.org/programs/jackie-robinson/jackie-robinson-1944-court-martial/)

According to Rosa Parks, her refusal to give up her seat was because she was ***exhausted of backing down****, not because she was physically exhausted.*

- Rosa Parks: My Story
Author Rosa Parks

What was traveling on a bus really like for black people, especially in the south?

White people that traveled by bus had seats in the front of the bus. Black people that traveled by bus had to sit in the back of the bus, behind white people. These guidelines were especially harsh in Montgomery, Alabama. Once the ten allotted seats in the front for white people were filled, the bus driver would force black people to get on up and move on back so that there will be space for other white bus travelers entering the bus to sit.

-Paraphrased from -
Hoose, P. (2010).
Claudette Colvin: Twice Toward Justice.
Square Fish: New York, NY

What did the '*corridors of power*' do as a solution to the Civil Rights Movement?

Please understand this one true fact. Not until the passing of the **Civil Rights Act in 1968** did black people receive full legal human and civil rights. Yes, not until 1968! This meant that it would be illegal to discriminate against black people on the basis of their skin color. These civil rights are to protect people from being discriminated on the basis of race, color, religion, gender, etc.

So, let's take a look back.

The **Civil Rights Act *of 1964*** was signed by President Lyndon Johnson acknowledging through law that *men equal under God* should not be discriminated in public places like restaurants, when they apply for a job, go to schools or in the event they try to stay at a hotel.

The Voting Rights Act of 1965 acknowledged through law the right for black citizens to vote (also known as '*black suffrage*') without discrimination.

To increase the effectiveness of the Civil Rights Act of 1964, President Lyndon Johnson acknowledged by law through the **Civil Rights Act of 1968**, fair housing for all and for all human beings to now be a part of the American way of life.

Unfortunately, these Civil Rights Acts rely on *voluntary compliance* and like I have mentioned earlier,

> *"The changing of the laws does not mean the changing of the hearts."*

Sadly, this implies that black people still experience prejudice and discrimination, despite these laws.

Many black men were disqualified from voting because of poll taxes and the literacy tests given.
What about the poor whites that couldn't pay the poll taxes and could not read or write?

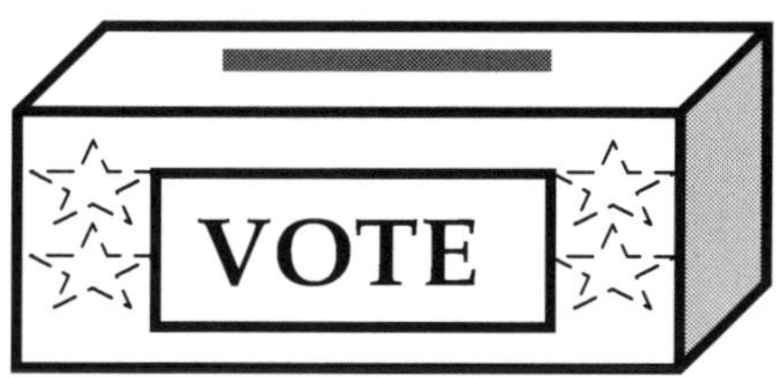

In 1870, the 15th Amendment outlawed racial discrimination when it came to voting rights. Nevertheless, especially in the southern states, black men were threatened or even killed if they attempted to register to vote.

This repulsion didn't stop here. Additionally, in an attempt to avert black men their now legal right to vote, new minimum requirements had to be met by US citizens.

Male citizens had to pass difficult literacy tests showing their ability to read and write, pay poll taxes and answer questions about the Constitution. But this plan impacted more than just blacks. It **disenfranchised** poor whites that could not read, write or even pay the poll tax.

So, in order to safeguard the voting rights for poor whites, the **'Grandfather Clause'** was created (white leaders needed the majority of whites to support this plan- the wealthy and the poor).

The 'Grandfather Clause' was an established law during the Reconstruction period with the purpose of denying **suffrage** (voting rights) to blacks, however it allowed poor whites to vote if they, their father or grandfather could vote prior to 1867.

Before 1867, blacks were unable to vote, so blacks did not have this privilege as poor whites did to circumvent taking these tests and paying poll taxes.

This was done to ensure blacks stayed behind and did not have a strong political influence. As a result, black people out of politics strengthened white peoople's political power so that they stay ahead.

(Note: Women could not vote until the passing of the 19th Amendment in 1920. Even still, black women were often discouraged from voting because of constant threats and abuse at the hands of white people that didn't want the black vote.)

(Source: African American Registry – AAREG
"Grandfather Clause Enacted"
https://aaregistry.org/story/grandfather-clause-enacted/)

What other silent and peaceful protest have we seen similar to the 1968 demonstration by Olympic runners Tommie Smith and John Carlos?

Colin Kaepernick is a former National Football League (NFL) Quarterback for the San Francisco 49ers. He is most famous for "taking a knee" during the U.S. national anthem to protest systemic oppression and police brutality towards black people. At a 2016 preseason game, he stated,

"I am not going to stand up to show pride in a flag for a country that oppresses black people and people of color. To me, this is bigger than football..."

Hurdle #7

Breaking Down Stereotypes

Questions to Discuss

How does segregation help reinforce stereotypes?

When people are segregated on the basis of race, what ends up happening is a **misunderstanding** of each other. Negative stereotypes begin to pervade people's consciousness as a result of limited exposure and inadequate personal experiences with people of other races.

Let's take a quick look back at the minstrels also known as performers in "blackface". If a white person (child or adult) has never had a personal relationship with or spoken directly to a black person, then it is easy for them to believe that black people are "buffoons or idiots" because of the image portrayed.

Segregation perpetuates racial stereotypes and makes it difficult for blacks to be represented positively when there aren't many counter images -of these stereotypes -provided.

How did Affirmative Action help everyone?

According to the *Stanford Encyclopedia of Philosophy* , **Affirmative Action** means positive steps taken to increase the representation of women and minorities in areas of employment, education and culture from which they have been historically excluded.

Historically, white males were the highest to be accepted into higher levels of learning and were the most likely to be hired for jobs.

President John F. Kennedy presented the term Affirmative action in 1961 to guarantee racial and gender diversity in education and employment without discrimination. It was enforced by President Lyndon B. Johnson in 1965.

Many argue that school acceptance should solely be based simply on merit and hiring should be simply based on qualifications; however black people who've had **equal** merits and were **equally** qualified were not given **equal** opportunities as whites.

Affirmative Action opened many doors as black people and women were given more opportunities to attend colleges and universities and also, many more were hired for jobs.

Critics of Affirmative Action claimed that it was reverse discrimination which led to its continual demise.

(Source: Teen Vogue
"Affirmative Action: What It Is and How It Works"
https://www.teenvogue.com/story/what-is-affirmative-action-explainer)

What is racism?

Racism is the belief that people of a certain race are inherently *superior* over people of a different race and exercising their power over people that are of a different race. Racism is also the belief that people of a certain race are inherently *inferior.*

Who would be considered a racist?

A person that is **racist** feels hatred and/or shows animosity toward other people that are not a part of his or her own race.

What is systemic racism?

Systemic racism refers to the *policies* and *procedures* that are set up to prolong racial inequity. (For example, the wealth gap, black unemployment, high interest home loans for black people, redlining, routine discrimination)

What is structural racism?

Structural racism refers to a system that can be social, economic or even political that are habitually practiced where white people have received *more opportunities* and black people have *less opportunities* on the basis of race. (For example, prejudice in school, media crime coverage, hiring discrimination)

Can you give me an example of institutional racism?

Sure! Let's take a quick look back to redlining.

A black person looking to purchase a home could have extreme wealth and an excellent credit score, however there were laws put in place by the federal government that prevented blacks from being able to buy property.

Structural racism actually became federal laws that white people had to obey unless they risked being punished themselves by the federal government. So whites were highly encouraged not to sell to black people and banks were urged not to finance home loans for black people. If they did, the federal government could take legal action.

This was simply a discriminatory behavior that turned into a law, better known as **institutional racism.**

Another example of institutional racism was the **G.I. BILL,** which was a law offering college tuition, low-interest home loans, among other things to veterans. However, not all veterans received equal benefits from this G.I. Bill.

This bill did help white veterans get more education opportunities and accrue more wealth, but this is not the same experience for blacks.

The individuals that prepared this law structured it in a way that individual states (as opposed to the federal government) had the ability to choose who would benefit from the G.I. Bill.

It was clearly known that segregated states would not allow black veterans to benefit from this bill. But the Federal Government gave states control anyhow.

This is yet another example of institutional racism where white people received more benefits and blacks received little to none. This is why white people are so far ahead because of benefits such as this one.

(Source: History.com
"How the GI Bill's Promise Was Denied
to a Million Black WWII Veterans"
https://www.history.com/news/gi-bill-black-wwii-veterans-benefits)

What is racial equity?

Racial equity is the allocation of society's ...

benefits

and

inconveniences...

that are not influenced by race.

If white people have a 400 year head start, how do you explain why there are some poor white people?

Simply put, the *'powers that be'* will ensure that most black people don't get ahead even if they have to use their own white people as ***collateral damage*.**

It's kind of like the *kamikaze*, which were Japanese pilots during World War II that used their airplanes as bombs to attack United States warships. They consequently killed themselves in the process. They destroyed their own life to be a sacrifice. These pilots knowingly knew what their suicidal responsibility was and how its purpose was to help Japan "win" and the United States to "lose".

However, in the case of the poor white people, they did not volunteer to be in the position they are in. So, in many cases they lose and the *'powers that be'* continue to win at the expense of everyone else.

Who does racism impact?

Racism impacts **everyone!**

Racist people believe that they are superior, which is obviously not a healthy way of thinking.

Racism..

offers opportunities

and

gives worth ...

to people based on an **outward appearance**

instead of their **intrinsic value.**

People that have been mistreated at the hands of racism can then, in turn, start to feel inferior, which also is not a healthy way of thinking.

So, this is how racism affects everyone.

In addition to how the *'corridors of power'* actually misuse their power, journalist Nikole Hannah – Jones put it this way,

"Racism is...
'You'll hurt white people
to hurt ***MORE*** *black people.'"*

- Nikole Hannah-Jones
Journalist behind New York Times Magazine's '1619 Project'

(By the way, I found this statement said by Nikole Hannah-Jones to be so profound that it was deserving of its own page. Go ahead. Let that sink in.)

What is the Infrastructure of America?

These **buildings** represent the United States of America.

Racism is the **foundation** in which the United States of America began.

This means that the infrastructure ...

or the frame...

or the foundation ...

of the United States of America began with *racist ideologies*: the idea that white people are superior to other races, also known as *white supremacy*. It has built a **<u>structure</u>** of behavior that consistently discriminates against black people.

The foundation is the most important <u>structure</u> of an entire building. It carries the weight of the building. It also keeps the structural *integrity* of a building together.

Maintaining the foundation is something that is certainly often forgotten and ignored because it is buried in the ground. However, ***cracks in the walls*** are a sign of a faulty foundation.

Now, if slavery, lynchings, convict leasing, sharecropping, redlining, experimentations, mass incarcerations and police brutality aren't enough evidence to prove there are *"cracks on America's walls"*, then I don't know what else will.

A flawed foundation is unstable and if nothing is done in good timing, things will only become much worse. So, chop-chop! Let's get it together!

Where did the 'N-word' come from?

The **'N'-word** is so offensive to me personally that I would just like to refer to it as the 'N'-word. However, some readers may not know what I mean by the 'N'-word, so to be clear, the 'N' word is the word 'Nigger'. This word was often used by white oppressors toward blacks in bondage.

This 'N'-word originally came from the Latin word 'Niger' which meant black. However, when Africans were taken into captivity at the hands of Europeans, this word 'Niger' quickly turned into 'Nigger'. This is a racial slur that has been used to hurt black people. When used, it implied that black people were ignorant, unsophisticated, worthless, etc... I'm pretty sure you get the picture.

The National Association for the Advancement of Colored People **(NAACP)** was created with the mission to "eliminate race based discrimination and ensure the health and well-being of all persons". The 'N' word in the form of 'Nigga' has been used heavily in the black community as a term of endearment. It has also gained a lot of popularity with its usage in today's music. For this reason, the NAACP organized a mock funeral to bury the word 'Nigga' from our vocabulary (2007).

Some will argue that black people are taking power away from the stigma that this 'N'-word has, which is why they use it. They

want to claim this word as their own and embrace it under a new meaning.
To many others, the 'N'-word is synonymous to the *all too familiar* racism – whippings, torturing, killings, separating of families and so forth.

It is my opinion that the use of the 'N-word' in any form or coming from any messenger – no matter his or her race- is harmful to the black community.

This word was literally beat over our ancestors heads like a stick to degrade them and it's as though some black people said,

"Hey, give me that 'N'- word stick so
that I can keep beating on our black people...

Since it is no longer popular for whites to say,
I'll disgrace us on behalf of all you racist white people.
Don't worry. I got this."

Basically, there are too many words in the English vocabulary that we can use to describe each other: buddy, comrade, pal, mate, homie, acquaintance, amigo and friend.

Our options are not limited, so we should *not* try to make this racial epithet a term of endearment when there are so many other, non-damaging and **affirming words** to commend one another.

Just think about all the stolen black people in chains, on the ships, working on the plantations and marching for black rights to not to be considered or called the 'N'-word. Think of them the next time you repeat it in song or before you think to have it roll off of your tongue in conversation.

(Source: New York Times
"Dictionary Will Revise Definitions of 200 Slurs"
https://www.nytimes.com/1998/05/03/us/dictionary-will-revise-definitions-of-200-slurs.html)

Why do you think some black people are active participants in hurting themselves and others that look like them?

White people made a huge investment of 400 years of degradation and subjugation of black people that they are still benefiting from. This is similar to **passive income.**

Passive income is making money while you sleep.

Passive income entails an upfront use of money for future profit.

Passive income also requires a lot of fostering, cultivating and development in the beginning stages for optimal success.

Passive income can be made with other people working in the trenches "for you" while you enjoy the benefits.

The beneficiary of passive income does not have to participate in the day-to-day operation after a while. They will continue to get paid after the work is done.

Let's take real estate for example. People can purchase real estate in the form of a house or a building and then rent it out to other people, while making huge returns on their investment.

Then there are also **royalties**-in the form of money-from *books for authors* or from *songs for writers*. These productive people put the hard work in the creative process and initial marketing. Eventually, they can enjoy the royalty that accrues most likely from the promotion of their product or service **done by other people** (bloggers, social media users, advertisers, etc.).

The upfront investment that white people contributed were things like:

*their decision to enslave Africans
*racist name calling
*making white physical features the standard of beauty
*persuading people to believe black features were the *complete opposite* of the standard of beauty
*promoting the false narrative that black people are inferior

*and basically acting upon their "white superiority"

Unfortunately, white people did an exceptional job in nurturing these attitudes so much that many black people started to take on these same negative opinions as their own. Please know, this is a typical result of being consistently disgraced.

It develops **shame** in a person that is fed so much negative images about who they are-or rather-who others say they are.

This shame will only continue to *grow* the more they are fed negativity as opposed to being fed positivity about the greatness they hold.

Because of this initial investment done early on by racist white people, black people may consciously or unconsciously hurt their own black community by:

*calling each other the N-word
* making fun of each other's "black" features
* perpetuating black inferiority by believing black people (like themselves) are second-rate
*and believing that in order to be successful they have to mold themselves into whiteness, which basically means to literally change one's own character, disposition and uniqueness to appeal to white people

These black people are simply responding to a system that created **stimuli designed** to destroy the self-image of black people. This ultimately influences the demise of black pride.

*"The **black skin** is not a badge of shame,*
*but rather a **glorious symbol** of national greatness."*

-Marcus Garvey
Black Nationalist Leader, Journalist, Orator
Started the *Universal Negro Improvement Association*
(UNIA)

"Young (black) people don't have hope...
because they look at the leadership... and they say,
'To get along in American society you have to be a sellout.
You have to put on a suit. Talk like a white man. Ask for what
white people want. Say what white people like ...
to be successful...'
Young black people don't see that as something they want to strive for. We want to be able to be who we are. Talk how we talk. Walk how we walk. Live how we want to live. And be producers and providers for our children in the future."

-Sister Souljah
Activist, Recording Artist, Film Producer,
Best Selling Author of
No Disrespect and The Coldest Winter Ever

Hurdle #8

The Impact of Slavery on Modern America

Questions to Discuss

What exactly do you mean that there is a 400-year head start?

Let's first delve into the fact that black people are the only ethnic group that was **forced** to come to America against their will. Every other ethnic group had a choice. America was established as the "land of opportunity" or some may even say the "land of the free", but this is a complete *contradiction.*

How can this be true with people owning other people as slaves? How can the ideal of freedom be a reality for only one group? One race? No one else? Just white people? How could they have made sense of this?

These liberating principles were a beautiful thing, but boy, the follow through sucked! It was awful! Inconsistent! And a complete flaw in our country's beginnings.

Enslavement of Africans being shipped to the **New World** (referring to the Americas) happened over 400 years ago. Most notably is the year 1619 when the privateer called the White Lion brought what many have said are the first African captives to the English colony of Jamestown, Virginia. This sea journey from Africa to the New World is called the **Middle Passage** which was a part of the Transatlantic Slave Trade.

African people that were enslaved lived in-*what would eventually become*- America longer than the existence of the established United States of America (1776). It's shocking, isn't it?

Despite literally being extremely instrumental in building this country, it's hard to understand how it is still possible that blacks experience astronomical challenges to this very day. This persistent struggle is largely due to the *systems* and *structural forces* at work that hold blacks on the lowest level of the **caste system.**

To be clear, the 400 year head start refers to the gap and disparity between black people and white people from slavery to present day. White people and black people were simply not given the same **equal access to opportunities.**

There are documented occurrences dating back over 400 years in which white people have exploited black people physically and mentally. In addition, American policies and laws were established that ***aided and abetted*** white Americans to having advantages and privileges that were not made accessible to blacks resulting in the 400 year head start.

It's not that white people worked harder than black people.

It's not that white people have some miraculous intelligence that supersedes black people.

This head start was birthed out of cheating, deception, immorality and a very evident contradiction in the Declaration of Independence: *"All men are created equal"*. White people had and still have a competitive advantage because they had a hefty head start.

And while they were getting

richer and richer,

and *educated and more* educated

and *employed and more employed,*

black people were subjugated to being oppressed.

But black people have made so many impressive gains and strides...**despite all of this.**

In what areas is there evidence of these gaps where a *racial caste system* seems to be maintained?

These gaps include, but are not limited to the **disparities** in:

*wealth

*education

*quality of neighborhoods

*quality healthcare (i.e. 2020 Corona Virus epidemic)

*workplace discrimination

* incarceration rates

* home ownership, etc .

Why don't black people just work harder to close these gaps?

Let's be honest here. No one has worked harder to live out the democracy we are all meant to have in America! No one!

"This is a staggering gap that **no amount** *of hard work will breach. It just simply will not be closed with hard work."*

-Tricia Rose
Internationally Acclaimed Scholar and Public Speaker.
Director of the Center for the Study of Race and Ethnicity in America at Brown University.
Award-winning author.

Why do so many blacks feel a void when it comes to knowing their black history?

Well, you have to understand that our ancestors were *physically stolen* from Africa and *the stories* of Africa were also *stolen.*

(Please check out Henry Louis Gates Jr.'s six-hour series on PBS entitled "Africa's Great Civilizations"
https://www.pbs.org/show/africas-great-civilizations/)

Why is there black on black crime?

"We have to start taking the **structural forces** *that got us here seriously. Police brutality and black on black crime is the product of the same thing. Somebody made a policy decision that certain people were going to live in certain communities and these communities will be invested in..."*

-Ta-Nehisi Coates
Author of Between the World and Me

"The more respected an African-American male youth feels, the less likely he will be violent ....

The opposite is also true...

The more disrespected he (an African-American) feels, the more likely he'll be violent."

-Dr. Joy Degruy
Author of Post Traumatic Slave Syndrome

How was the '*culture of violence*' in poor black communities created?

"African 'American life in this country has been violent from the moment we got here in 1619.

There's always been a cultural violence... A cultural violence that has been put upon us...

We have **250 years of slavery...**

We have **150 years of 'Jim Crow',**
which is violence ...

and during that period, we have <u>redlining</u> to make sure we herd certain people into certain neighborhoods ....

We **deprive** *those neighborhoods of certain resources...*

We **deprive** *those neighborhoods of jobs...*

We create what sociologist call criminogenic conditions and then we're shocked that the murder rate is high.

Why are you shocked?"

-Ta-Nehisi Coates
Best-selling author of <u>Between the World and Me</u>

How does *the system* work to cause friction between black people?

Dominoes are set up to be knocked down. They are put in strategic positions by a person with power, so that they can fall. And not just fall. But topple on top of one another to ensure most, if not all, other dominoes collapse.

If you were to ask the 3rd domino in a row, *"Who knocked you down?"*, it will most likely say, *"The 2nd domino knocked me down"*, or if dominoes were falling from the other direction, they may say, *"The 4th domino knocked me down."*

But if the 3rd domino had a better vantage point with a clear view of what was actually going on, they would see that the 2nd and/or 4th domino were not the the *cause* for the dominoes' inevitable plunge.

The culprit was that finger pushing the dominoes down in the first place. Unfortunately, since it **appears** that the 2nd or

4th domino were the initiators, the 3rd domino quickly blames them.

In retrospect, it is easy for black people to criticize those closest to them (most likely other black people) for their inconveniences, difficulties and setbacks, rather than noticing that the push for the dominoes to fall, came directly from the '*corridors of power*'.

(Note: The finger pushing the dominoes represents the '*corridors of power*' or some may call them the '*powers that be*' which are the highest level of authority mostly occupied by white people. The dominoes represent black people that were intentionally positioned to topple over. **But remember. Some dominoes don't fall.**)

Practically speaking, in the 1980s, ***allegedly*** someone from the '*corridors of power*' gave crack cocaine to black people to distribute and sell to other black persons in their community (typically low income communities in the inner city). It was extremely profitable for black dealers to sell this drug and this drug also gave users a 'high' (a euphoric feeling of pleasure), so it became very desirable.

The dealer gets addicted to making money and the drug user gets addicted to drugs because some will argue they are suffering from a "sickness".

This **crack epidemic** essentially destroyed many lives in the black community. Violence increased, more children were placed in foster care, families were shattered, many were arrested in the black community and far too many died.
We can also look at the **music industry** and virtually see the same thing. The *'powers that be'* also have a lot of control in regards to what type of music and artistic representation will be fed into the world.

Music producers are motivated to market music that represents the black community in a negative light because essentially... this is what sells. But it's all by design.

They are pushed to feed into the many stereotypes and instead of listening ears being inspired to be their best through music, they often receive harmful messages that one day they will want to imitate.

Again, black people can harm their own communities through how we represent ourselves. But, if we take a step back, we will clearly see that this was the plan all along.

This is my opinion on how *the system* works to cause dissension and friction within the black community.

(Note –In an *University of the District of Columbia* interview,
Dr. Jeff Menzise calls this model the *Domino theory*.
He is the author of Dumbin' Down:
Reflections on the MIS-Education of the Negro)

Who is more likely to commit *property crimes* like burglary, larceny, theft, motor vehicle theft, shoplifting, arson or vandalism?

Individuals that are **unemployed** are more likely to commit property crimes (as opposed to violent crimes) where a criminal hopes to acquire money, property or another form of profit.

To put it plainly, when job opportunities are available, the crime rate is likely to go down.

People that may not have an opportunity for employment, for whatever reason, may find it difficult to live a standard life, so they are more likely to live a life of crime.

"...a vast majority of people who are incarcerated come from poor communities, particularly concentrated in those of color. Therefore, those most vulnerable to the formal criminal justice system are also subject to the brunt of the abuses of the informal criminal justice system, bearing the mark of "convict" for the rest of their lives."

(Source: Wharton- University of Pennsylvania
- Criminal Records and Unemployment
https://publicpolicy.wharton.upenn.edu/live/news/2071-criminal-records-and-unemployment-the-impact-on)

This mark of "convict" takes away the opportunities for employment since many businesses only want to hire people with a clean record. Consequently, people that have committed a crime become repeat offenders because no one will hire them and they stay unemployed.

What is the connection between mass incarceration and the Jim Crow Laws?

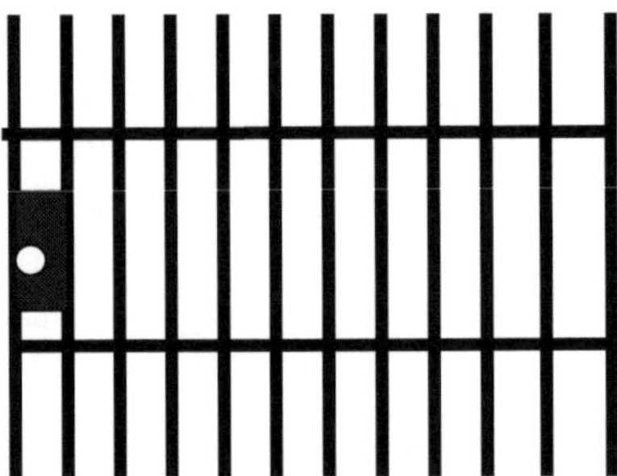

When the War on Drugs was highlighted in the mid 1980s, if a person had possession of **5 grams** of crack, they would be sentenced to 5 years in jail.

Crack is the drug that the **black community** was heavily exposed to.

On another note,
if a person was in possession of **500 grams** of powder cocaine, they would receive the same 5 years sentencing in jail.

Powder cocaine was a drug that the **white community** used.

The crazy thing is, crack and cocaine are essentially the same drug, however blacks were sentenced way harsher: 5 grams versus 500 grams. This helped towards the mass incarceration of black people, especially black men.

You may not realize it, but there is a strong connection between **mass incarceration** and **Jim Crow laws.** They both promote legal discrimination.

The discrimination from the past has basically taken on another form. Police disproportionately search young black men and are more likely to imprison them for non-violent drug offenses.

Upon release, they are stripped from their right to vote, rejected from educational opportunities and denied employment due to background checks.

- *Paraphrased from* -
-Alexander, M. (2020)
The New Jim Crow: Mass Incarceration in the Age of Color Blindness. New Press. New York, NY.

Who "benefits" from mass incarceration?

The mass incarceration of black people has not only stunted

the advancement of the black community, but it has also provided cheap labor for private companies. Mass incarceration is highly profitable for prisons that needed to have as many prisoners, as possible, to get paid the most money. This also allowed prisons to be able to ensure *workers at prisons* are able to keep their jobs. The more bodies a prison fills, the more money the prison makes.

Economics. It's all about economics at the expense of so many black lives.

(Check out:
https://www.nytimes.com/paidpost/netflix-13th/plantation-to-prison.html)

"Once the system of mass incarceration began to grow, it became quickly apparent that a lot of money could be made."

-Michelle Alexander
Author of The New Jim Crow

Why is there a disproportionate amount of black students, particularly boys that are in Special Education?

The truth is that there are many students that need to be in **Special Education** to receive essential services for their specific situation. However, studies have shown that black boys have been excessively suggested for Special Education classes.

This classification can hurt black students' records, files, future opportunities and self-esteem, especially if they didn't need to be placed outside the general classroom. It also adds to the stereotype that, as a black boy, you are not capable of **mainstreaming.**

Some will even argue that this is just another form of segregation. Hmmm...You decide.

(Source: The Edvocate
"Black Boys In Crisis by Matthew Lynch"
https://www.theedadvocate.org/black-boys-crisis-many-special-education/)

But black people have had a black president. You guys should be happy, right?

Yes, we had a black president. Many have even said that we are post racial because **President Barack Obama** was successfully elected into office. But nothing could be further from the truth . Racial biases are still breathing and living strong today as in the past.

A black man in the highest office position possible does not have the ability to change the evilness in people's heart. The achievement of this one black man does not mean blacks as a whole have made it. We have a long road ahead of us.

We've had hundreds of years of slavery, endured prejudice and unfair policies against the betterment of blacks that we are still recovering from, and eight years can't change that.

The victories some black people have accomplished are not reflective of so many *more* blacks still languishing in poverty, in educational disparities or even the wealth gap. The day that we have all made progress as black people, is the day when we can say… **"Yes, we've made it!"**

Why do blacks continue to struggle as compared to other races?

Martin Luther King said it best when he explained that there is no other ethnic group that has been enslaved legally on American grounds. He said that white people have also made the black color a stigma. At the time when slaves were freed, they were **left with nothing** for their livelihood. But "European peasants" received acres of land when they came to America so that they could create a strong financial foundation.

So, there was land to give, but white people refused to offer land to the newly freed black people.

Dr. Martin Luther King wants to make sure that white people don't overlook the **legacy of slavery** and segregation.

Whites will tell blacks to,

"Lift up your bootstraps,"

but blacks don't even have any boots as a result of oppression.

– Dr. Martin Luther King
Civil Rights Leader

I will also add that when people experience **trauma**, they go to a therapist or counselor for rehabilitation. Now, I don't know too many more things worse than the trauma that must have been caused by chattel slavery.

These enslaved people did not receive treatment after being emancipated.

Their children did not receive treatment.

Nor did their children's children.

If we make an effort to ignore or make light of slavery and racism without truly confronting it, then what we end up doing is taking on the trauma and then passing on that same trauma to our children. And so the cycle of trauma still lives on until we receive the guidance and assistance to overcome these past tragedies.

We must **face the ugly** truth of enslavement. We have to start at the core and not just look at our symptoms.

What is one of the first steps black people need to make to begin to *heal* from this trauma?

"We need to figure out who we are...where we came from, and whose shoulders we're standing on...
We are the descendants of captured free people.
And we have lived out a legacy of not knowing and not understanding our ***intrinsic nobility****...worth...value...as a people. And until we understand that, we cannot expect ... anyone moving forward to be healthy."*

-Dr. Joy DeGruy
Author of Post-Traumatic Slave Syndrome

As a white person that *did not* enslave black people, why do I feel like I am taking the blame for what my ancestors did or didn't do?

To put it simply, white people **still benefit** from the oppression of black people. And black people **still suffer** from this oppression done by white people.

Black people today are *still hurting* from the systemic injustices done to our ancestors from the first day of slavery >>> through the Reconstruction period >>> through Jim Crow >>> through redlining >>> and through the Civil Rights era.

White people are *still benefiting* from the oppression of their ancestors starting from slavery >>> through the Reconstruction period >>> through Jim Crow >>> through redlining >>> and through the Civil Rights era.

No one is directly blaming you for what your ancestors may or may not have done (or at least I am not personally). Hopefully, you are able to recognize the advantages you have today at the expense of the exploitation of black people.

Why do you write about race?

Well, to be honest, when people see me, they see the black skin that I am in. To some, it can be threatening and/or an undesirable trait. To others –if I'm being honest- my black skin can draw people in, because this skin I am in is just so exquisite. **Off-the-chart beautiful!** And I am more than proud to be blessed to wear this badge of strength as my covering.

However, race has the ability to influence disparities. Our differences have allowed some people to believe that they are intrinsically superior to others and that other people are fundamentally inferior. *Those are who we call racist.*

So, I write about race to make it clear that our human eyes may be flawed in this type of thinking, but if we have the wisdom of putting on God's lens, we will see that we are all one. No one is greater than another. No group is better. God sees us all the same and we should too. *This is called being an antiracist.*

Can you share examples of *implicit biases* that occur today?

#1

I have a friend that applied for a job with a prestigious company. Not only did she submit her resume, but she sent in two resumes! Both resumes were completely identical, except for the name.

Just so you know, her real name is a typical **"black"** sounding name and she knew that she would probably not get a call back for an interview if they believed she was black. For that reason, she decided to test her theory and submit a second identical resume with a typical **"white"** sounding name.

And as she expected, she received correspondence for an interview as a response to her resume with the "white" sounding name and never received a response back from her identical resume with her "black" sounding name.

Same resume.

Different names.

Implicit bias.

#2

Dr. Joy DeGruy is the author of the book entitled Post Traumatic Slave Syndrome. During a presentation, she read a news caption regarding Hurricane Katrina in New Orleans that occurred in 2005. This following news caption was next to a picture of a black person and it stated:

"A young man walks through chest deep flood water after ***looting*** *a grocery store..."*

Another news caption next to a picture of white people stated:

"Two residents wade through chest-deep water after ***finding*** *bread and soda at a local grocery store..."*

So, do you see anything odd with each caption?

"Same event.

Same water.

White people.

Black people...

These people can't be perceived as looting. They're white people. White people don't loot... I'm (referring to the news) going to steal the social conscious by letting you know...
don't forget...
this (the black person) is a looter."

-Dr. Joy Degruy
Author of Post Traumatic Slave Syndrome

What is one way the *myth* that blacks are inferior has perpetuated in our society?

It is a *grievous error* for people to believe certain myths about black people. And it's so unfortunate that white people are not the only ones guilty into believing certain fallacies perpetuated throughout society (for example, the myth that black people are inferior). Black people have been taught that they don't have a past or a future. White people are often told directly or indirectly that they are *special*, which ultimately gives them a sense of entitlement.

"..If the world does it to you effectively enough...you become a collaborator... an accomplice of your own murderers... They think it's important to be white ...then you think it's important to be white. They think it's a shame to be black...then you think it's a shame to be black."

-James Baldwin
American Novelist. Poet. Activist.

Other ethnic groups and even black people themselves have fallen victim to believing untruths and this creates a poor image of blacks that are simply not true.

My hope is to teach a black past that comes from **strength** and a black future that births **perseverance.**

University of Washington's professor, Dr. Robin DiAngelo, spoke about the ***power of the story.*** She explained how the way a story is told can yield a different effect.

For example, she stated that many people celebrate Jackie Robinson for being the first black man to 'break the color line in sports'.

"The story of Jackie Robinson is a classic example of how whiteness obscures racism by rendering whites, white privilege, and racist institutions invisible. Robinson is often celebrated as the first African American to break the color line and play in major-league baseball. While Robinson was certainly an amazing baseball player, this story line depicts him as racially special, a black man who broke the color line himself.

The subtext is that Robinson finally had what it took to play with whites, as if no black athlete before him was strong enough to compete at that level.

Imagine if instead, the story went something like this: "Jackie Robinson, the first black man whites allowed to play major-league baseball." This version makes a critical distinction because no matter how fantastic a player Robinson was, he simply could not play in the major leagues if whites—who control the institution—did not allow it. Were he to walk onto the field before being granted permission by white owners and policy makers, the police would have removed him."

- Dr. Robin DiAngelo

DiAngelo, R. (2018). White Fragility: Why It's So Hard For White People To Talk About Racism. Beacon Press: Boston, MA.

(Note: It has been documented that **Moses Fleetwood Walker** was actually the first black man to play in the Major Leagues back in 1884, well before Jackie Robinson in 1947.)

(Source: MLB - A True Pioneer http://mlb.mlb.com/mlb/history/mlb_negro_leagues_profile.jsp?player=walker_fleetwood)

What is one reason urban schools in predominantly black communities aren't doing so well?

Schools require educators, teacher's aides, supplies and other resources *minimally* to function as a well-run institution.

School funding is often decided by the **property taxes** of the homes that are in the neighborhood. A school in a more affluent neighborhood will receive more funding, classroom aides, resources and materials as compared to a school in a poor black community. Wealthy kids continue to benefit from state aid, while poor kids don't benefit as much.

This is why schools in poorer communities highly depend on the philanthropy of others.

I am a teacher.
What do schools serving the black community need to be successful?

Lisa Delpit is the author of Multiplication is for White People and she made a profound statement that *"white babies and black babies are not born with an achievement gap."* She believes that it takes **academic press** and **social support** to have a successful school and that you cannot have one without the other.

Academic press is translated as academic rigor, high level thinking, demanding curriculum and lessons connected to common core.

Social support is translated as knowing your students (for instance, understanding the community they live in), connecting the curriculum to the community and the students interests (for instance, teaching history that looks like them), creating a sense of safety, building a relationship with students and parents (Don't just call parents when a student is misbehaving. Contact parents even when a student is doing well.) and making students feel that they **belong** by ensuring students feel connected to their teachers and their school.

"You can't have social support without rigor and you can't have an academically rigorous school and no social support."

– Lisa Delpit,
Author of Multiplication is for White People

I would also like to add that school success happens when schools have materials and resources available to them. Computers are highly used in school and needed to complete homework assignments nowadays, but if certain students don't have access to a computer at home, this can be difficult.

Students have the option of going to a local library, but this is just an added challenge for students who may not live near a library or can't get to a library without parental support.

However, there are many understanding teachers at schools that will allow students to complete computer generated work during their recess, lunch or afterschool, so it can get done. It just takes a village of supportive family and educators.

It's also important to note that when a teacher doesn't **believe in their students**, students are less likely to **believe in themselves.** As a teacher, please make sure that your students hear you use positive affirmations such as calling them a *'scholar'* or a *'winner'* so that there is no doubt in their mind that you think of them any less.

What are *racist ideals* as opposed to *antiracist ideals*? "

"Racist ideals *suggest that certain racial groups are superior or inferior, better or worse than others...*

Racist policies *yield racial inequality...*

Racist people *are people who are expressing racist ideas or are supporting racist policies with their actions or inaction.*

Antiracist *ideals suggest that the racial groups are equals...*

Antiracist policies *yield racial equity.*

To be antiracist is supporting antiracist policies with their actions."
(For instance, supporting reparations, quality healthcare for all, etc...)

-Ibram X. Kendi
New York Times Bestselling Author
Author of
How to Be an Antiracist and Stamped From the Beginning

What is white supremacy?

"White supremacy has been for the last centuries…(since its inception), a handout system **for** *white(s)* **to** *white folks. It's a system of entitlement, such that it's not recognizing merit. It's not recognizing talent. It's not recognizing hard work. It's recognizing your ability to assimilate into whiteness and to claim power over people of color: black folks and indigenous people."*

-Crystal Marie Fleming, PhD
Writer and sociologist who researches racism.
Author of How to be Less Stupid About Race

Since blacks are behind in having access to opportunities, do blacks have to work twice as hard?

To imply that black people have to work twice as hard (if not more) as white people in order to reach the same goal can actually be a double-edged sword. On one end, a child being told they have to work twice as hard may receive this advice as saying that they aren't good enough or even competent enough, so that's why they have to work twice as hard.

On another end, the fact of the matter is when people know the truth of their starting point, then they can position themselves to do the extra that's required to be successful. We can't allow ourselves to be deceived in thinking that we are all on the same **starting line.** So often times you will hear black parents advising their children about this reality. If someone is giving **100%**...give **200%**. And this looks like:

*putting on a button down shirt to work when others are wearing t-shirts

*putting on a mask (smile) when you really want to frown

*being the first one at work or possibly being the last to leave work

*sitting in front of the classroom as opposed to sitting in the back

*turning in assignments way before the deadline (as long as it is meticulously completed)

*and bringing in additional resources or sharing information that supports your teacher's lesson, so that there is no doubt in their mind that you are more than ready and willing to learn.

Regrettably, far too often, black people have to work harder to be seen as equally competent as their counterparts from other nationalities. This is because of the negative narrative that is widespread about black people as a whole. We need to do all we can to create a **counter-narrative** that tells the truth of our incredible abilities.

How have governmental policies broken down the black family?

First of all, the stability of the black family has been under attack ever since they were **stripped** from their African homes, away from their African family members. And then once enslaved, their family members were sold to other slave owners ... again stripping them apart.

However, the black family stood the test of time and were united even under oppression.

Most recently though, some believe that **one culprit** of the breakdown of the black family directly connects to **welfare** programs under Aid to Families with Dependent Children (AFDC) and their no "man in the house" rule. To put it simply, this is a welfare program where poor families (headed by a single mom) were provided financial assistance, however it required that no male head of the household (or any man) can live or even be present in the household. In surprise visits, if a male was found in the household of the female recipient, financial support would decrease or be cut off totally.

This seemed to be a significant gateway in the direction of the **weakening** and subsequent **destruction** of the black family as a unit.

Abraham Lincoln is famous for stating,

"A house divided against itself cannot stand."

The same can be said when referring to a once strong, stable family that has unfortunately been broken or divided:

A family that is divided ***-as welfare rules, mass incarcerations and killings of black males has done-*** makes the black family unit not as strong as it could be, creates confusion instead of unity and makes it more difficult for the black family to "stand".

History doesn't lie.

This is not a coincidence. The more separated, split and divided (physically and mentally) black people are, the more difficult it is for them to get ahead.

Blacks seem to play victim and I think they just need to work harder and stop depending on whites to help them get better.
Don't you agree?

Blacks don't play victim.

They have been victimized!

Let's have a look at the semantics of the word victim. A victim is somebody hurt. A victim is somebody killed. A victim is somebody harmed. And a victim is someone that has been duped into believing lies.

Blacks have been and *still* are victimized by racial discrimination, but are *still* committed to thriving despite this.

Unfortunately, some people of various races (even fellow blacks) may believe that black people as a whole are not advancing as much as they should, due to a ***victimhood mentality*.**

So, do blacks have a reason to see themselves as being victimized?

I say, yes!

But does this mean that blacks should sit around and do nothing while waiting for a handout?

Certainly not!

Although restitution and restoration is highly deserved, I believe that black people, even knowing their hurtful past or current day experiences, should use this pain and turn it into something that strengthens them, making them more determined than ever to prosper. This, by the way, is the purpose of this book.

I would also like you to consider that *the system* is designed for certain individuals' hard work to receive **MORE NOTICE** and be considered **MORE SIGNIFICANT** than the hard work of other certain, specific and particular individuals.

There has been much evidence of blacks working extremely hard to lift themselves up, however there was always a way their efforts were thwarted or destroyed (Please research the *Black Wall Street Massacre* in the Greenwood community).

I recognize that I have an advantage.
What can I do with my privilege to help underserved black communities?

Having an advantage and certain **privileges** comes in many colors.

Whether you are a prosperous black or white person (or any other ethnicity), use your privilege to enhance conditions for black people – men, women, boys and girls – in their community by offering your time doing community service, providing donations and/or by supporting black businesses.

You do not make good use of your privilege if you use it to obtain fame or wealth for just yourself. Privilege should be used to generate equity where prejudice has been evident.

When we share our resources, we are not simply ***dividing*** these resources. We are ***multiplying*** these resources amongst an entire community that will eventually benefit everyone.

"We have to ***BE A HOPE****. Having hope is too detached. You have to be a participant. You have to be an agent. You have to keep on pushing... be a force for good... courageously bearing witness no matter the circumstances because you are trying to live a life of integrity until the good Lord brings you home."*

-Cornel West
American Philosopher, Social Critic and Author

What does supporting the black community look like?

Supporting the black community looks like:

*utilizing black businesses
*offering black students specific trade skills to middle and high schoolers in urban communities
*being informed about the happenings in these neighborhoods
*looking at history to avoid repeats
*being a philanthropist by donating your time, funds and/or supplies to schools in need
*teaching the truth about black history to the youth
*and exposing the bad and ugly while also sharing the many successes and victories in America's true history.

During a speech for **TIME MAGAZINE**, author Jason Reynolds challenges the audience to simply acknowledge people of color. I strongly believe that what he stated is pivotal in what is necessary in supporting the black community effectively. He challenged the audience to recognize people of color and . . .

"Not just the ones that are **convenient** *for you to love. Not just the ones that are on a college track. Not just the ones you feel safe around. The ones that are complex, challenging... who talk all kinds of ways. All of them deserve our* **love.** *They sit in your classrooms and they're in your neighborhoods . . .*

It don't matter if we're next unless we are looking out for the 'next next'.
My mama always said,
'You can't be a king unless you can be a king maker!'
Young people . . . you are truly the antidote to hopelessness."

- Jason Reynolds
New York Times Best Selling Author
STAMPED: Racism, Antiracism, and You

Nikki, what is one aspect you want your readers to take from this book?

As much as I didn't want to know the horrifying truth about my black history, I needed to know the truth. I couldn't learn and appreciate all the victories without learning about the many battles.

I have learned that we have to face what has been done to our predecessors and how it still impacts black America today. We can't suppress the trauma and turn a cold shoulder to it as if it never happened.

I want my readers to be ***liberated*** in knowing who was instrumental in the construction of building the United States of America. Blacks were more than enslaved. They were country builders!

For Your Information: The White House in Washington D.C. was built by slaves. The US Capitol in Washington D. C. was built by slaves. Wall Street in New York was built by slaves. Trinity Church in New York was built by slaves. The University of North Carolina was built by slaves. Monticello in Virginia, the home of Thomas Jefferson, was built by slaves. Mount Vernon in Virginia, home of George Washington, was built by slaves. This is just to name only some of the magnificent contributions black people 'built' in this country.

(Source: "15 American Landmarks that were Built By Slaves" https://www.businessinsider.com/american-landmarks-that-were-built-by-slaves-2019-9#monticello-in-virginia-14)

Nikki, what do you want your non-black readers (especially *white readers*) to fully comprehend after reading this book?

First and foremost, this book is not about creating white guilt. This book is about education that teaches the **good, the bad and the ugly**... as long as it's telling the truth. Far too long and generation after generation, we have been given the pretty wrapped **"gift"** of deception and now it's time to unwrap these lies and start opening up to the truth.

"The first step toward tolerance is respect and the first step toward respect is knowledge."

-Henry Louis Gates Jr.
American Literary Critic. Harvard University Professor. Author. Historian. Filmmaker.

One truth that white people, in particular, need to understand is that they have what is called ***'white privilege'.*** White privilege does not imply that white people have never struggled. White privilege also does *not* mean that a white person did not work hard for their accomplishments. White privilege is *having more* opportunities, control and influence than any other racial group. But many will deny the power that they have by just being white. This is why I want to make it crystal clear what I mean when I say white privilege because white privilege is inherent. It's simply part of the nature of America.

So, what does white privilege look like?

* *White privilege* is *not* habitually being stopped by the police because you "look suspicious".
* *White privilege* is consistently seeing a vast amount of positive representation of other white people on television (Superheroes, doctors, princesses, lawyers, teachers, etc.).
* *White privilege* is when non-white neighborhood home prices increase in an event a white person moves in the area. This implies that a white person's mere presence brings more value

than anyone else. The opposite occurs when black people move into a white neighborhood: Property values seem to decrease.

* *White privilege* is being expected to be smart.
* *White privilege* is having descendants that are able to pass down their accumulated wealth (most white people, not all).
* *White privilege* is being a young, white rambunctious student and not being suspended or kicked out of school impulsively because of poor behavior. White privilege receives more sympathy and patience.
* *White privilege* is committing a crime and not being convicted or receiving a shorter sentence than non-whites.

"Just as people of color did nothing to deserve ... unequal treatment, white people did not **"earn"** *disproportionate access to compassion and fairness. They receive it as the byproduct of systemic racism and bias."*

(Source: Tolerance.org
"What is White Privilege, Really?" by Cory Collins
https://www.tolerance.org/magazine/fall-2018/what-is-white-privilege-really)

My hope is that white - and frankly - other non-black people will get a better understanding of the structural inequalities that exist in this world that continue to impact black Americans today and across the world. Instead of ignoring, running away or trying to separate themselves from this painful reality, I want white people to recognize it, admit it is real and maybe even grieve with black people about the black experience.

And finally. **Do something.** Say something. Be a support. Get to know someone that is black on a personal level to understand who they are and discredit any stereotypes.

Just think about it? Really... put on your thinking caps. Had black people been given the freedom to just be our extraordinary selves, everyone would have benefited from more of our ingenuity. The fact that black people have come as far as we have is simply a marvel, despite the various forms of bondage put upon us.

Only God knows how far ahead black people could be today without the constant barrage of interruptions. But unfortunately we live in a world where people feel they can't get ahead without stepping on someone else's back.

And this is why we should all advocate for **social justice.**

Social justice is the distribution of wealth, opportunities and privileges within a society.

Social justice equals human rights.

Social justice equates to equality.

And we need to work toward social justice to see America live by what it was founded to live by. Although this country has substantial evidence going ***against*** the very liberties it stood for, I am optimistic that we *can* do better.

The systems that make laws and are highly influential are controlled by the *'corridors of power'* which are heavily occupied by white people. If more white people, black people, brown people...no matter what color, find themselves in positions of influence, with this **knowledge** of *structural inequalities* and genuine **concern** for social justice, then and there is when change can be had.

So, although this information can bring about some uneasiness, be willing to have an open ear and share this new knowledge with your acquaintances.

Nikki, what realization do you want your *black readers* to fully comprehend after reading this book?

I want my readers, specifically my black readers, to understand that there have been ***many labels*** put upon the entire black race. It is our responsibility ***not to internalize*** these negative beliefs as our own.

While a multitude of people (whites and even blacks) think black people are the culprit to "America's problem", we have to understand that we are not the problem. Racist policies are the problem.

For one, there would have been no need for any type of **insurrection** had it not been for America's decision to ***enslave*** black people. Yet still, people referred to blacks as being rebellious and defiant when black people were simply resisting being treated less than human. Again, black people were not the problem. The problem was legalized slavery.

Moreover, ***white racism*** gave rise to the **Black Power Movement** in the 1960s and 1970s. This movement highlighted pride in the black race because of the consistent discriminatory practices held by law enforcement and the '*corridors of power*'.

Again, I repeat, black people were not the problem.
The problem was white people acting upon their racist beliefs.
Simply put, don't believe the hype.

"We are working *for a world where Black lives are no longer systematically targeted for demise.*
We affirm our humanity, *our contributions to this society, and our resilience in the face of deadly oppression."*

-Black Lives Matter
An organization whose mission is to build local power and to intervene in violence inflicted on Black communities by the state and vigilantes.

Nikki, what do you expect people to do with this information after reading your book?

Ephesians 5:11-14 says,

"Have nothing to do with the fruitless deeds of darkness,
but rather **expose** *them. . .*
But everything exposed by the light becomes visible . .
This is why it is said:
'Wake up, **sleeper . . .' "**

Frankly, I want my readers to wake up!

I want my readers to understand that black people are descendants of Africans that **were enslaved** and weren't *slaves by nature.*

I want my readers to become more conscious about the legacy of slavery that still affects blacks in America to this present day.

My hope is that after grappling with the truth and realities of the black experience, that this knowledge will spread to those who will go to action the best way they see fit.

Whether I have sparked an interest in someone to learn more about their black history so that they can teach their children, I feel I have done my job.

Whether I have provided an *easy to understand* resource **empowering** young readers about the resilience of their people, I feel I have done my job.

Whether I have encouraged someone to be more bold in responding to racist comments said by their friends or family members, I feel I have done my job.

My purpose with this book is to ensure that any person reading it can't say that they didn't know. If we want to celebrate the victories of America, then we have to be willing to confront the catastrophes as well.

Education is powerful and when we know better, we do better!

"Oh, That's Why!"

There were just some things I didn't quite understand, but upon much exploration I now find myself often saying,

"Oh, that's why!"

For one, I could never understand how my mother and other black mothers like her could clean and cook the rancid smelling pig intestines called chitterlings. They even had the nerve to devour them. In their mouth. And swallow.
As if they actually......Tasted......Good.

But then I learned, our ancestors that were enslaved were forced to eat the left-over meat -
the spare meat that white slave owners didn't want. The ox tails, the chicken necks, the pig's feet and the gizzards. These foods are part of a tradition passed down from generation to generation. Now, I completely understand and can say,

"Oh, that's why!"

Likewise, for the life of me I couldn't understand why black people had such distrust for police. These were men and women that were always kind to me. When they were called to help, they always assisted, smiled at me and even gave me a sticker. But this is not everyone's experience.

Historically, police have not been so kind to black people. From time to time, they have joined in the storm of oppression, racial profiling, beatings, false accusations and shootings of unarmed blacks. And unfortunately, these brutalities didn't just happen in the past. They happen today. Right now. It may be happening even as you are reading these words. Now, I would never suggest running from the police or disrespecting them. Our job is to do everything "right" within our power, so that we can make it home...alive.

But, I can now honestly say with clarity, I understand. I understand that black people have hard feelings toward police because they've been hurt... They run - even if they are innocent - because they are afraid of being killed.

"Oh, that's why!"

I was just a freshman in college when I didn't fully grasp why the OJ Simpson verdict was a day of celebration for black people. It was as if the team competing at the Super Bowl *-that every black person was rooting for* - won. That's how excited everyone was.

It was because he represented all the black people that were unjustly convicted of crimes prior to him. Whether he was actually guilty or not, black people felt a sense of vengeance- although our hearts sympathized for the victims and their family. I didn't get it then. I just thought we were supporting him because he was black. He was someone that looked like us.

But in fact, it had less to do with OJ and more to do with the entire black race feeling they have been persecuted for way too long ,and so I say,

"Oh, that's why!"

Now let's dive into a topic that seems to puzzle so many. Why do some black people tend to spend so much money on things that don't appreciate in value?

Some blacks, not all.

And why is it that black people that have low income may also own a two hundred dollar pair of sneakers, a luxury car, 'hair-did',. 'nails did', 'everything done', suited and booted, but may not even have a few hundred dollars saved in their bank account?

Some blacks, not all.

This behavior is not indicative of the entire black race, however there's enough of this happening to question... "Why?"

Well, I discovered that this is yet another connection to how the legacy of slavery impacts black people today. From day one in America, black people were told that they were inferior, subhuman, ignorant, worthless and poor in every sense of the word. These weren't just words spoken audibly to black people through radio, music, television or word of mouth. Stereotypical messages were also perpetuated through newspapers, magazines and how black people were treated. Since they have been treated as insignificant, they *may* want to challenge this narrative by buying things that appears to bring them status.

"Oh, that's why!"

Lastly, it has never bothered me, but touching a black woman's hair is pretty much a BIG NO-NO! I know that it is pretty tempting since our hair can do so many impressive flips and poofs, and curls and whips. So, I get it. However, what I couldn't figure out was why black women would get so annoyed when someone, especially from another race, touched their hair.

I am a touchy-feely person myself. And I get so curious that I just want to touch...touch...touch. But it's not normally on a person. It might be to pet a dog. And black women are not dogs, but may be led to feel as though they are seen as an animal on display at a petting zoo. The unsolicited touch or even asking permission to touch a black woman's hair –to some - is offensive, given our history.

Black people were made to be a spectacle. Out of the norm. An anomaly. By who? By white people. They put black people on display for entertainment... literally. Like at a zoo, in a cage display. Or 'circus', on a stage to be exhibited. And yes, these things really did happen. So, the next time someone attempts to touch a black woman's hair and I hear a smack on the hand, I can confidently say,

"Oh, that's why!"

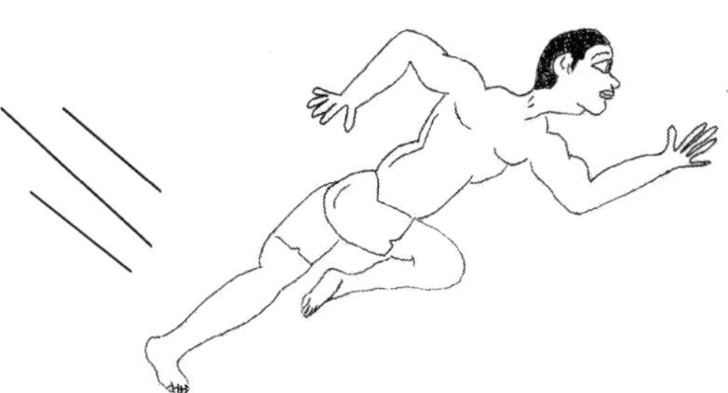

Parents and Teachers!

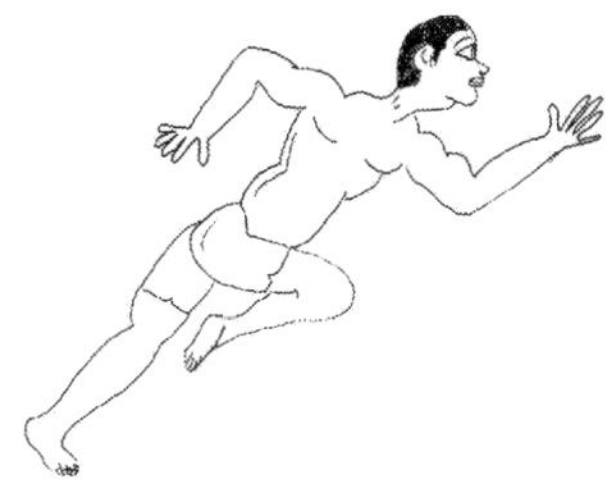

This book only *skims the surface* of various experiences in American history that has hindered or tried to prevent black advancement. But obviously, the tenacity and grit of black people could not be halted. So, please have your son/daughter or students:

(1) choose one landmark event stated in this book
(2) research it in more detail
(3) write about it
(4) and/or use their artistic ability to create a reflection of what they have learned

Thank you for choosing to educate!

"...We rejoice in our **sufferings**, *knowing that suffering produces perseverance, and* **perseverance** *produces* **character** *and character produces* **hope."**

-Romans 5:3-4

"Do you not know that in a **race**
all the runners run,
but only one receives the prize?
So run that you may obtain it."

-1 Corinthians 9:24

Made in the USA
Coppell, TX
25 May 2020

26443409R00180